PLANT LIFE OF THE GREAT BARRIER REEF

PLANT LIFE OF THE GREAT BARRIER REEF AND ADJACENT SHORES

A.B. Cribb & J.W. Cribb

University of Queensland Press

ST LUCIA • LONDON • NEW YORK

First published 1985 by University of Queensland Press
Box 42, St Lucia, Queensland, Australia

Typeset by University of Queensland Press
Designed by Paul Rendle
Printed in Hong Kong by Silex Enterprise & Printing Co.

Distributed in the USA and Canada by the University of Queensland Press,
5 South Union Street, Lawrence, Mass. 01843 USA

Cataloguing in Publication Data

National Library of Australia

Cribb, A.B. (Alan Bridson), 1925–
    Plant life of the Great Barrier Reef and
adjacent shores.

    Bibliography.
    Includes index.

    1. Marine flora – Queensland – Great Barrier
Reef Region – Identification. 2. Coastal flora –
Queensland – Great Barrier Reef Region –
Identification. I. Cribb, J.W. (Joan Winifred),
    1930–   . II. Title.

581.9943

Library of Congress

Cribb, A.B.
    Plant life of the Great Barrier Reef and adjacent
shores.

    Bibliography: p.
    Includes index.

    1. Coral reef flora – Australia – Great Barrier Reef
Region (Qld.) – Identification. 2. Island flora –
Australia – Great Barrier Reef Region (Qld.) – Identification.
3. Coastal flora – Australia – Great Barrier Reef
Region (Qld.) – Identification. 4. Great Barrier Reef
Region (Qld.) I. Cribb, J.W. (Joan Winifred)
II. Title.

QK453.C74   1985   581.9943   84-3704

ISBN 0 7022 1984 3

Contents

Illustrations

Preface

The Great Barrier Reef is Australia's greatest natural tourist magnet and an inexhaustible source of scientific interest, so it is not surprising that it has been the subject of numerous books, which have varied greatly in depth of coverage. It is the corals and other associated animal life for which the Great Barrier Reef is justly famous, and all the books hitherto published on its natural history have been devoted mainly or exclusively to its animal life and geological structure. However, in the plant life of the area, both terrestrial and aquatic, there is a great deal that is of interest and beauty, and it is hoped that this volume will help to reveal some of it and fill a gap in the available literature. The work is directed mainly to the interested nonprofessional but it may be of use also to some scientists who have interests beyond their own specialized fields.

The flora of the cays is limited, often numbering less than fifty species, so it has been possible to include reference to most of the species found on those islands. On continental islands and along the mainland shore there are some species which are also widely distributed away from the shore but, although not specially characteristic of the Great Barrier Reef area, are nevertheless likely to be noticed by visitors to the area. In such cases a somewhat arbitrary decision has been made on whether or not to include the species.

Both mangroves and sea-grasses comprise relatively small numbers of species, and it has been possible to note the majority of species occurring in the area. On the other hand, there are some hundreds of attached marine algae, many of them microscopic; in this work are included only those larger species which have been judged common, conspicuous or notable in some other way.

It has been our experience that interest in a subject is greatly stimulated by the availability of information on that subject, and we hope that this will prove to be the case with the plants of the Reef.

We are indebted to staff of the Queensland Herbarium for assistance with determination of some flowering plants, to the National Parks and Wildlife Service of Queensland for permission to collect and camp in areas of the Great Barrier Reef which are National Parks, and to Miss L. Danaher for typing the manuscript.

Foreword

Plants are fundamental to all life on earth. They use sunlight to initiate a flow of energy in the form of food upon which almost all other forms of life depend.

In the oceans of the world, the role of green plants seems far less obvious than on land, but is nevertheless equally vital. In the open oceans drift myriads of tiny free living plants. These are the plankton, converting sunlight and basic raw materials into living tissue, growing and in turn being consumed by a vast range of animals, including the mighty filter feeding baleen whales.

The first written records of coral reefs spoke of magnificent coral gardens. The low bushy and taller tree shaped structures, with brightly coloured "flowers" and butterfly-like fish all reinforce this initial impression. It was only later that the true animal nature of the coral polyp, more akin to anchored jelly fish than to flowering plants, was revealed.

In some ways more recent discoveries have taken us full circle. The mystery of how these tiny limestone secreting animals could produce mountain chains, like the 2000 kilometre long Great Barrier Reef, from the relatively low nutrient input available in captured and ingested organisms, has been at least partly solved. They do not live and grow unaided.

Within their bodies live millions of tiny single-celled green plants (close relatives of the free swimming algae of the oceans) which coexist within the coral polyps' tissues, using the energy from sunlight to capture carbon dioxide for the production of organic material and limestone and incidentally providing the rainbow range of colouration we appreciate in the "coral gardens".

So the beauty and complexity of coral reefs, just as much as rainforest ecosystems, rely on green plants. Even the massive coral foundations of growing reefs are not purely the result of coral skeletons. Often inconspicuous, but universally present, are plants, green and brown coralline algae, which feed large numbers of grazing animal species and produce a tough limestone skeleton which eventually makes its contribution to the growing reef.

Despite the fundamental importance of plants on coral reefs they have often been ignored, and many remain to be described in scientific terms.

Not all the plants associated with coral reefs are marine. There are at least fifty-six permanent vegetated coral cays in the Great Barrier Reef area. Once a piece of land remains consistently above sea level the first land plants take hold, and in time a low forest may develop, producing the idyllic landscape for which coral islands are renowned. The Reef area also contains many high or continental islands and the vegetation they support is more closely allied to the plant communities of the mainland.

Because of the scale and complexity of the Reef even a substantial research effort leaves much unexplored. We hope that this book, by bringing some of the scientific work into the hands of the general reader, will also serve to encourage further study by both the amateur and the professional.

The acknowledged need for further study was one factor influencing the establishment of the Great Barrier Reef Marine Park. This very proper desire to preserve the Reef for study needed to be balanced against the wishes and rights of the general public to visit and enjoy the Reef. It was also necessary to consider the interests of those who make their living in Reef waters, for example, as fishermen or in the tourist industry. The need to ensure that these interests did not conflict with each other or with the conservation of the Reef, led to the development of the marine park concept. The Marine Park aims, by zoning and management, to provide for the protection, wise use, appreciation and enjoyment of the Great Barrier Reef in perpetuity.

I commend this book to you in the hope and belief that it will enhance your enjoyment and understanding of the Great Barrier Reef.

Graeme Kelleher
Chairman
Great Barrier Reef Marine Park Authority
which assisted this publication

1   *The coral reef*

Coral reef structure

The Great Barrier Reef Province, the greatest system of coral reefs in the world, stretches along the Queensland coast for approximately 2000 km from Lady Elliot Island to Torres Strait. True barrier reefs occur only north of Cairns, but the practice of referring to the whole area as the Great Barrier Reef is well established. Within this area numerous reef types have been recognized but there are probably three basic types. Fringing reefs border the mainland shore and the shores of continental islands. Because of the appreciable freshwater runoff to which they may be subjected, coral development on such reefs is often less vigorous than on barrier or platform reefs. Barrier reefs are narrow reefs running approximately parallel with the coast at the edge of the continental shelf. Platform reefs are usually roughly rounded or elliptical, flat-topped structures arising from the continental shelf at some distance from its edge. Some of these reefs support cays such as Lady Elliot Island, Heron Island, Green Island and Low Isles, the areas usually visited by people whose main aim is the viewing of coral. Platform reefs in which there is a depressed area forming a lagoon have been termed "lagoonal platform reefs".

A platform reef such as the one on which Heron Island is situated can be divided into several regions. Although there is some variation from reef to reef, a basic pattern can usually be recognized. The intertidal area adjacent to the cay may be divided into four main regions: beach, reef flat, reef rock rim and seaward platform.

Beach

Unconsolidated beaches are mainly without attached algae, but in many cays part of the beach material has become cemented, by a process not fully understood, to form beach rock. Such rock is colonized mainly by a thin, sometimes slippery layer of Blue-green Algae.

Beach rock formation is a surprisingly rapid process, and on some Pacific islands weapons from World War II have been found embedded in it. On Wreck Island in the Capricorn Group there is an iron ring firmly cemented into the beach rock, possibly part of the wreck to which the island owes its name.

Beach rock on Masthead Island

Reef flat

The reef flat is an enormous tide pool, the water being dammed over it by the reef rock rim. It can often be divided into two parts. The inner reef flat, often submerged to a depth of about 30 cm at low water, supports scattered coral clumps with a relatively rich algal growth on dead coral surfaces. In the outer reef flat, coral clumps of larger size have linked up to form a platform broken by numerous irregular pools often up to 75 cm deep. Coral is usually better developed here than on the inner reef flat but fleshy algae are relatively sparse.

Reef flat from the shore, Masthead Island

Aerial view of Masthead Island reef

Reef rock rim

Enclosing the reef flat is a rim of reef rock, usually 35–100 m wide, its upper part no more than a few centimetres above the upper limit of coral growth on the reef flat. The reef rock rim is often divisible into two parts. Its upper part is the

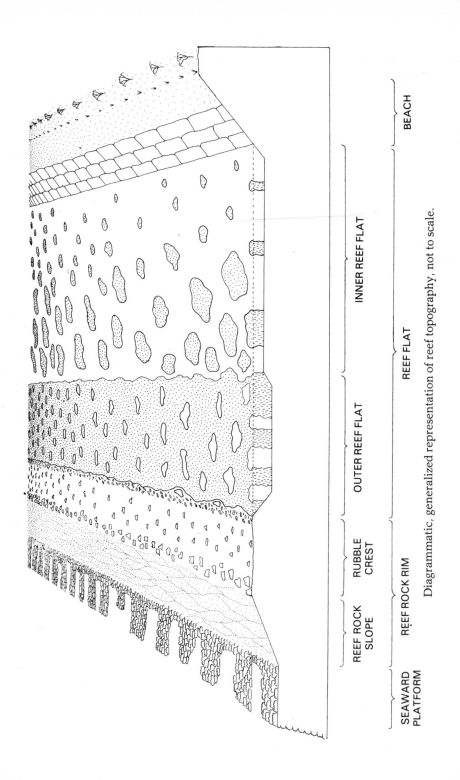

BEACH

REEF FLAT

INNER REEF FLAT

OUTER REEF FLAT

REEF ROCK RIM

RUBBLE CREST

REEF ROCK SLOPE

SEAWARD PLATFORM

Diagrammatic, generalized representation of reef topography, not to scale.

Shallowly terraced reef rock slope with rubble crest in distance on right, Tryon Island

rubble crest, typically an area of heavy rubble deposition, the fragments varying from finger-like pieces to reef blocks or boulders a metre or more high. Seaward of the rubble crest and not sharply distinguished from it is the reef rock slope, 0.5–1 m in vertical extent, a gently sloping expanse of reef rock covered with a yellow-brown sand-binding turf of numerous species of algae. In some places at the eastern ends of reefs this expanse is so smooth that one could ride a bike blindfold over it. However, mostly it is marked by shallow, meandering terraces, not over a few centimetres high, which link up to form an irregular network; particularly near the western ends of reefs the area may be densely pot-holed or ir-regularly eroded.

Seaward platform

The outermost part of the intertidal reef is the seaward plat-form, a relatively narrow strip, usually 5–40 m wide, either sloping gently seaward or almost horizontal. At its seaward edge it may drop precipitously or dip gradually to deeper water. On some reefs the seaward platform is dissected at right angles to its length by gulches 2–4 m wide, resulting in a spur and groove system. This is typically an area of rich coral

Seaward platform, Hoskyn Island

growth. The heavily calcified encrusting algae, or lithothamnia, also are common here but fleshy algae are poorly
developed.

Coral reef algae

Coral reefs are remarkable for the enormous richness and diversity of their animal life, and it is this animal life that most visitors to the Great Barrier Reef come to see. By contrast, the algal, or seaweed, vegetation is relatively poorly developed, being mainly small in stature and low in species diversity. One coral reef worker, Sylvia Earle, has even written that "perhaps the most striking aspect of plant life on a coral reef is the general lack of it".[1] Nevertheless, algae are present in greater diversity than is at first apparent and have several important functions in what is regarded as the most complex of all marine ecosystems.

Although it is usually the corals which provide the main building materials of coral reefs, some algae also play an important part. These are the species of Green and Red Algae which have calcified tissues. Among the Green Algae, species of *Halimeda*, particularly *H. opuntia*, are the most important. These algae are not important reef builders at their site of growth but, as they break up, their calcified fragments are transported to other areas and, in some reefs, are important constituents of beaches and lagoon sediments. More important reef builders are the calcified Red Algae sometimes known as lithothamnia. These algae, most of them forming stony, pink crusts, are important builders at their site of growth, not only providing firmly attached bulk, but also giving stability to the dead coral which they commonly overgrow. Lithothamnia are found in most parts of coral reefs but are often best developed on the seaward platform, the outermost part of the intertidal reef. On some strongly wave-beaten reefs it is the lithothamnia rather than the corals which are mainly responsible for the seaward advance of the reef.

Important as algae are in reef construction, a few also contribute to its destruction. Nearly all illuminated calcareous material such as mollusc shells, dead coral and even the skeletons of some living corals are penetrated by various

1. Sylvia A. Earle (1972), The influence of herbivores on the marine plants of Great Lameshur Bay, *Natural History Museum Los Angeles City Science Bulletin* 14: 17–44.

filamentous algae. Calcium carbonate is dissolved ahead of the growing filaments, and eventually growth becomes so dense that the material takes on a blue-grey or green-grey colour. There is little definite information on the extent to which these algae lead to breakdown of the calcareous material, but the density of penetration in many cases leaves little doubt that they are important in the recycling of calcium carbonate and the provision of space for new growth.

On land, it is mainly the flowering plants which are the primary producers of organic material which supports, either directly or indirectly, all animal life. In the sea, it is the algae and the relatively few species of marine flowering plants which form the basis of the food chains in which the many thousands of animal species are involved. Unicellular, planktonic algae carried freely in the water currents are responsible for some of this productivity but the waters in which coral reefs are found are low in nutrients and support only an impoverished phytoplankton population. Some workers have even likened coral reefs with their abundant life to oases in a desert. Under these conditions the attached algae of coral reefs are particularly important as primary producers. On some reef flats at certain times of the year there may be large quantities of Brown Algae. For example, at Heron Island during spring and early summer there are large quantities of *Chnoospora implexa, Colpomenia* species and *Hydroclathrus clathratus*. However, in general, the quantities of algae present on coral reefs are small compared with those found in cooler waters. Nevertheless, productivity of coral reefs is very high. This high productivity coupled with small bulk at any one time is partly accounted for by the heavy fish grazing which occurs on some parts of the reef. For example, when the reef rock slope, occupied by a low turf of algae, is shallowly submerged it is often possible to see shoals of dozens of Parrot Fish and Spine Foot moving over the area, heads down and tails often out of the water, mowing the turf as effectively as a lawnmower trims a lawn. While there is not a large bulk of algae present on the reef rock slope it seems to be an area of high productivity. It can probably be likened to a regularly mown lawn which does not contain as much plant material as a similar area of shrubs but nevertheless produces a greater quantity of plant material in a given time.

There is a group of unicellular algae, the zooxanthellae, which play a major role in the growth of coral. These algae are found within the polyps of all reef-building corals and within the tissues of animals of some other groups such as the sea anemones and the clams. The association is one of mutual advantage. The coral benefits by having much of its waste materials removed by the algae. So efficient is this removal that one author has written of zooxanthellae as the animal's algal kidneys. The algal partner benefits through the assured supply of nitrogenous and phosphatic compounds which are in short supply in the surrounding water. Although coral polyps trap planktonic organisms, at least some corals derive some of their nutrients from material synthesized by the algae. The algae also have a profound effect on the rate of calcification by corals; in corals from which zooxanthellae have been removed calcification rates have dropped as low as one-tenth of the normal rate. So, in the absence of zooxan-thellae, growth rates of reef-building corals would be appreciably reduced and it is unlikely that coral reefs as we know them today could exist.

2   *Seaweeds*

The algae comprise a group of plants, predominantly aquatic in habitat, which lack flowers and reproduce, in some cases in a very complicated fashion, by means of spores. Most have not developed the elaborate conducting systems which, in the flowering plants, enable water and other substances to be moved quickly from one part to another. Marine representatives are generally referred to as seaweeds, and the freshwater representatives denigrated as green slime.

They are a very diverse group and, whereas the flowering plants all belong to the one major group or division, nine or more divisions make up the algae, varying from one-celled microscopic plants to some cold-water representatives about 60 m long which form submarine forests. Several characters are used in the classification of algae into divisions, one of the most important being pigment composition. Members of all groups contain the green pigment chlorophyll but, in addition, there is a group of pigments which is characteristic for each division of algae. The predominance of a certain pigment or group of pigments commonly gives the representatives of a division a distinctive colour, and so several of the algal divisions, in addition to their scientific names, are often given common names based on colour, for example, Division Cyanophyta (Blue-green Algae), Division Chlorophyta (Green Algae), Division Phaeophyta (Brown Algae) and Division Rhodophyta (Red Algae). These are the main divisions in which noticeable algae occur and are the only ones dealt with in this account.

While most Green Algae are green and most Brown Algae are brown, Blue-green and Red Algae are often not true to name. Although the distinctive complement of pigments is always present, the proportions of each may vary so that Red Algae, particularly when growing in well-illuminated positions in the tropics, are commonly any colour other than red, and may be green, fawn, olive, purple or almost black. Such variation in colour may make identification of an alga as a member of a particular division a matter of considerable difficulty for anyone without a close familiarity with the algae. There are several characters in addition to pigment composition used in the classification of algae into divisions but these involve the use of laboratory facilities, and this account aims at dealing mainly with characters which can be detected with the naked eye or with the aid of a hand lens.

Division Chlorophyta (Green Algae)

Acetabularia caliculus   Mermaid's Wine Glass

This distinctive plant has a slender stalk 2–5 cm high with a whorl of lightly calcified wedge-shaped rays at its upper end. These form a disc or shallow cup, about 5 mm across, which is responsible for the attractive common name.

Development at first is entirely within some calcareous substrate such as a shell or piece of dead coral. As the erect branches grow out they produce whorls of branched hairs which are progressively shed, and it is only the whorl of sac-like branches, topped by another whorl of hairs, which persists. The plants may occur singly but often there are dense groups of several dozen arising from a shell such as a whelk.

Acetabularia kilneri is a more robust species with caps about 15 mm across. In the Heron Island region the only representatives of the genus are dwarf species with stalks no more than 3 mm long and discs only a couple of millimetres broad.

In Indonesia, a species of *Acetabularia* has been used in folk medicine to treat gall stones and kidney stones. It has been

Acetabularia caliculus (Mermaid's Wine Glass)

suggested that this use may be based on the fact that the basal part of the plant has the ability to dissolve the calcareous material it penetrates.

Boergesenia forbesii

This interesting and beautiful alga usually occurs in groups of bright-green, club-shaped and often curved vesicles up to about 5 cm long, looking something like an elongated green grape. There are no cell walls within the vesicles, and its firmness is due solely to the pressure against the outer membrane of the sap it contains.

Boergesenia forbesii

Boodlea composita

The filaments of *Boodlea composita* branch profusely in all directions, becoming attached to other branches they happen to meet. In this way is built up a loose, lime-green clump, crisp and fragile, and often breaking up easily when handled. Water drains instantly from a clump when it is lifted from the sea, causing a sudden change in hue. The clumps, varying from small flecks to masses 20 cm across, are prominent on some reef flats mainly during the cooler months.

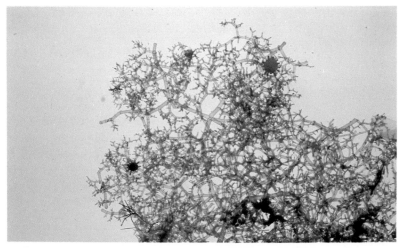

Boodlea composita

Bryopsis indica   Feather Weed

Prostrate filaments give rise to a dark-green cluster of often several dozen erect branches 3–7 cm high. Along two opposite sides of the upper part of these branches are neatly ordered and graded lateral branches which give the fronds a delicate feather-like appearance. There are no cross walls so

Bryopsis indica (Feather Weed)

the plant is a continuous tube. In the Capricorn Group this alga is found mainly on the seaward platform.

Caulerpa

All species of *Caulerpa* have a creeping axis attached at intervals by root-like rhizoids, and producing erect green branches from the upper side. Some grow mainly in sand while others are generally restricted to solid substrates. The central cavity, crossed by numerous microscopic strands of wall material, is continuous throughout the plant, so an injury is likely to lead to draining of some of the contents leaving the plant with a washed-out appearance. Among the various species there is a bewildering variety of form in the erect branches; even within the one species the form may be greatly influenced by the environment so that, in some cases, parts of the one plant growing on the upper and lower sides of a coral boulder may at first appear to belong to different species.

Caulerpa brachypus　　　　　　　　　Leafy Caulerpa

The erect branches are flattened and leaf-like. One small form with branches 3–4 mm wide often has the blade once or

Caulerpa brachypus (Leafy Caulerpa)

twice forked, while another more robust form, with blades about 1 cm wide and 2–8 cm long, often has small marginal teeth.

Caulerpa cupressoides   Cypress Caulerpa

This species typically grows in sand on the reef flat, the radiating, prostrate branches often spreading over an area of a square metre or more. Erect branches are usually forked two to six times and are densely clothed with small, overlapping, roughly cylindrical branchlets with sharp tips. In shaded plants these branchlets may be in three rows. A resemblance between these crowded appendages and small, overlapping leaves of the cypress is responsible for the *cupressoides* part of the name.

Caulerpa cupressoides (Cypress Caulerpa)

Caulerpa lentillifera   Bubble Caulerpa

The erect branches are densely clothed with globose vesicles, about 1.5 mm broad, borne on short conical stalks. These vesicles snap pleasantly when bitten. *Caulerpa lentillifera* is one of the edible species of the genus and is on sale in some markets of South-East Asia.

Caulerpa lentillifera (Bubble Caulerpa)

Caulerpa mexicana

Found on both sand and solid substrates, the erect branches of this species are pinnate, with the closely placed branchlets either straight or sickle-shaped. It has the same general form as *Caulerpa sertularioides* but the branchlets are distinctly flattened and much broader, being 0.3–1.2 mm wide.

Caulerpa mexicana

Caulerpa nummularia

The erect branches of this species are shortly stalked discs 3–7 mm across, with smooth or serrate margins. In some plants there is a series of up to four stalked discs, each arising from the margin of the disc below. This diminutive species is widely distributed but is perhaps best developed in the algal turf of the reef rock rim where it sometimes forms a close mat of overlapping discs.

Caulerpa nummularia

Caulerpa racemosa   Sea Grapes

This species exists in several varieties and forms and is one of the most common and variable species on the Barrier Reef. The branchlets clothing the erect branches are more or less club-shaped.

   In the Philippines one variety is cultivated as a salad vegetable and eaten with vinegar or salad dressing. It may not have immediate appeal to many Western palates but, if approached with an open mind, many will find it to have an interesting and even pleasant flavour. Another variety is mildly toxic, has a peppery taste, and may cause some numbness of the lips and tongues of those eating it; however, even this variety is eaten sparingly in the Philippines.

Caulerpa racemosa (Sea Grapes)

Caulerpa serrulata

The erect branches are forked several times, flattened to varying degrees, coarsely toothed and twisted. The degree of twisting may vary considerably in the one plant, well-illuminated parts being tightly twisted and grey-green, while shaded branches may show only slight twisting and be bright green.

Caulerpa serrulata

Caulerpa sertularioides   Feather Caulerpa

Slender, almost hair-like branchlets clothe the erect branches on two or occasionally three sides to produce feather-like fronds up to 5 cm high.

Caulerpa sertularioides (Feather Caulerpa)

Chlorodesmis fastigiata   Turtle Weed

There is probably no more striking alga on the Reef than Turtle Weed. Among the generally fawn to yellow-brown algal cover, the plant stands out because of its brilliant green colour.

The dense tufts consist of repeatedly forked filaments, up to about 10 cm high. Any slight water movement will cause the lax tufts to move freely; as a falling water level exposes the clump, the filaments are draped to show their bases which are paler and yellowish.

If fingers explore a clump of this alga, a hard object, cushioned by the filaments, may be detected. This can be gradually worked out and will be found to be a speckled yellow and green crab, *Caphyra rotundifrons*, well camouflaged among the green filaments where it characteristically lives.

Although commonly known as Turtle Weed, it seems doubtful that this is an important turtle food. It is rare to find

Chlorodesmis fastigiata (Turtle Weed) and the crab *Caphyra rotundifrons*

signs of its being grazed. When chewed it has a grassy taste soon followed by an unpleasant bitterness which may deter marine grazers.

On some reefs, a second species, *Chlorodesmis major*, is common. Superficially this appears almost identical with *C. fastigiata* but is a little larger and coarser and there are filament constrictions evenly placed above every forking while the constrictions in *C. fastigiata* are at slightly different distances above the forking.

Codium spongiosum   Green Sponge Weed

As the Latin name suggests, this alga has a sponge-like appearance. The heavy bottle-green clumps, often fist size or larger, are irregularly lobed and contorted. In spite of its fairly solid nature it is composed entirely of filaments. The outer club-shaped branches of these filaments are not united but are turgid and closely pressed against each other to form a palisade which gives a firm outer surface.

Another, less common, species is *Codium geppii*. This has repeatedly forked branches 2–4 mm in diameter, often with the branches uniting where they cross so that an intricate prostrate clump is built up.

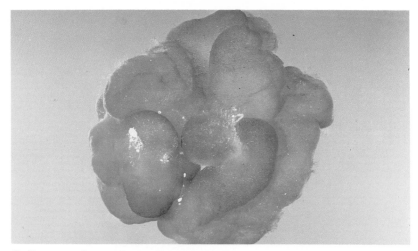

Codium spongiosum (Green Sponge Weed)

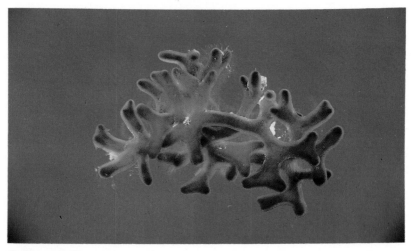

Codium geppii

A pale halo often seen surrounding *Codium* when in the water is caused by the presence of colourless hairs borne near the ends of the "clubs".

Species of *Codium* have been used for food in some areas, both raw and boiled, but we find this vegetable rather less than enjoyable.

Dictyosphaeria cavernosa   Green Bubble Weed

Green Bubble Weed at first forms a rigid, green, hollow structure up to about 4 cm wide, made up of a single layer of large cells up to 3 mm across, clearly distinguishable with the naked eye. The convex outer walls of these cells give the surface a pebbled appearance. Old plants often break open to form an irregular cup or plate.

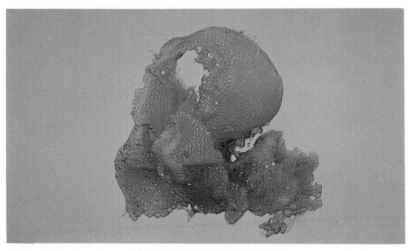

Dictyosphaeria cavernosa (Green Bubble Weed)

Dictyosphaeria versluysii (Grey Bubble Weed)

It is this seaweed which "went wild" at Kaneohe Bay, Hawaii, following various disturbances to the environment, including the discharge of sewage effluent into the bay. With this stimulus, the alga became exceptionally vigorous, overgrowing and killing large quantities of coral and helping to destroy what had once been a coral reef of exceptional beauty and richness.

A closely related species, *Dictyosphaeria versluysii* (Grey Bubble Weed) also is common on the Great Barrier Reef. It may be distinguished from *D. cavernosa* by its solid rather than hollow structure and often by its grey-green colour.

Enteromorpha clathrata   Green Guts

Plants of *Enteromorpha* are branched green tubes. In some areas they reach 30 cm or more in length and are obviously tubular, but on the Reef plants seldom exceed 3 cm in height and only microscopic examination reveals the hollow centre. *Enteromorpha* is common on beach rock, particularly during winter, and often on shells and coral fragments near the base of the beach. It is often the first alga to colonize newly available intertidal surfaces, such as clumps of coral dislodged by cyclones. Although edible and once used for food in various parts of the world, the Reef plants of *Enteromorpha* are mostly too small to be gathered for this purpose. Anglers use strands of *Enteromorpha* as bait for Black Bream.

Enteromorpha sp. (Green Guts) fringing pool in beach rock

The plant responds with vigorous growth to the fertilizing effect of domestic sewage.

Halimeda

Halimeda is a distinctive tropical alga named after a daughter of Halimedon, mythical Greek king of the sea.

The plants form branched chains of discs or cylindrical segments and are always calcified to varying degrees. This calcification makes some of them important reef builders, and the fragmented segments comprise a large part of the sediment of some lagoons. Bleached plants are often seen cast up on the beach, their limy skeletons pure white and relatively durable. The following are among the several species found along the Great Barrier Reef.

Halimeda cylindracea

This species is unusual among Halimedas in having cylindrical or bead-like segments 1–4 mm broad. The fairly

Halimeda cylindracea

regularly forked branches reach a height of about 15 cm. *Halimeda cylindracea* also is one of the few species to form a sandy "tuber" about 3 cm broad and penetrating the sand of the reef flat for up to 12 cm.

Halimeda macroloba

Plants of this species are heavily calcified, with dark-green discoid segments, 1–2 cm in diameter. As with plants of *Halimeda cylindracea* there is a massive sand tuber penetrating the floor of the reef flat.

Halimeda macroloba

Halimeda opuntia

The flattened segments of this species vary from elliptical to kidney-shaped or distinctly three-lobed, the form often varying considerably in different parts of the one plant. Segments are often crowded into dense clumps, less conspicuous than their commonness would suggest because of their often grey-green colour. *Halimeda opuntia* is a heavily calcified plant, and is the most important reef builder among species of this genus.

See also in chapter 6, "Flotsam".

Halimeda opuntia

Halimeda tuna

This is a very common species of the reef flat, with flattened fronds and kidney-shaped to irregularly rounded discs

Halimeda tuna

1–3 cm across. It is relatively lightly calcified and so is often of a brighter green than some other species. *Halimeda discoidea* is a closely similar species, distinguishable from *H. tuna* with certainty only by microscopic characters, although its identity can sometimes be guessed at on the basis of its very weak calcification and dark-green colour.

Microdictyon obscurum   Sea Gauze

Microdictyon's crisp but fragile green membranes up to 6 cm across occur in shaded places, usually on the undersurfaces of coral clumps. With good eyesight it is just possible to detect that the membranes are actually fine nets marked with a series of veins. A lens quickly reveals the delicate beauty of this plant.

Microdictyon obscurum (Sea Gauze)

Neomeris annulata   Caterpillar Weed

Although only 1–2.5 cm tall, Caterpillar Weed is distinctive. It grows as curved cylinders 1.5–2 mm in diameter, chalky white below and a bright lime green above. The calcified reproductive bodies in the lower part of the plant are cemented together in transverse rows. Another species, *Neomeris van-bosseae*, has the reproductive bodies free from each other.

Often growing with these species on the reef flat or in pools on the rubble crest are several related Green Algae – up to

Neomeris annulata (Caterpillar Weed)

three small species of *Acetabularia* less than 2 mm in diameter, and small firm green spheres of *Bornetella capitata* and *B. nitida.*

Udotea argentea   Mermaid's Fan

Udotea argentea is generally found growing in sand, where it is attached by an elongate mass of closely woven rhizoids. At the apex of a distinct stalk is a fan-shaped grey-green blade,

Udotea argentea (Mermaid's Fan)

sometimes irregularly lobed. Calcification of the blade gives it a fair degree of rigidity.

Ulvaria oxysperma
(Monostroma oxysperma)

Pools and shaded crevices in beach rock are the usual habitat on the Reef for this species. It forms extremely delicate, green membranous sheets, ruffled and folded, and only one cell thick. During summer it is usually seen as inconspicuous green flecks, but during winter may form sheets up to 8 cm long.

Species of *Ulvaria* are closely related to the Sea Lettuce (*Ulva lactuca*) and, like it, have been used as human food in various parts of the world.

Ulvaria oxysperma

Valonia ventricosa   Sailor's Eyeballs,
                                           Dragon's Eggs

This alga forms a rounded or egg-shaped structure up to 3 cm across, something like a very firm green grape with a blue-green sheen. It usually nestles in shaded crevices between dead coral branches or occurs on the undersurface of coral

Valonia ventricosa (Sailor's Eyeballs)

boulders. Apart from a few small cells near its base the whole plant consists of a single enormous cell. Its remarkable rigidity is due not to the structure of its wall but to the pressure of the sap it contains; if punctured by a pin this sap may squirt out like the jet from a water pistol. Such treatment, of course, kills the plant, so should not be carried out indiscriminately.

Division Cyanophyta (Blue-green Algae)

The Blue-green Algae form the most primitive of the major algal groups, and are regarded by some as bacteria.

Hormothamnion enteromorphoides

Not the most attractive of the algae on the reef flat, this species is sometimes present in large amounts, growing as wispy tufts of blue-green or bottle-green microscopic filaments up to 15 cm long, streaming in the current. Growing loosely attached, usually to old algae, the tufts are exceptionally slimy and very delicate, tending to fall apart when handled. In the lower parts of the tuft the filaments may become somewhat interwoven and catch sediment, giving the impression of a loose stem.

Hormothamnion enteromorphoides

Microcoleus lyngbyaceus   Mermaid's Hair

Great variation exists among specimens of this species; the plants are filamentous, variable in diameter, with the coarser filaments roughly the thickness of human hair. In some specimens the filaments occur in a loose tangle, in others they are spread out in a mucilaginous layer. Plants may be of almost any colour, but chiefly are blue-green, olive, brown, red or purple.

One of the snapping shrimps, *Alpheus frontalis*, uses the alga to build its home, weaving the filaments together to form a tube up to 15 cm long in which a pair of the shrimps live.

Microcoleus lyngbyaceus (Mermaid's Hair) woven into a tube by the shrimp *Alpheus frontalis* (removed from tube)

Oscillatoria erythraea
(Trichodesmium erythraeum)   Sea Sawdust

After his experience on Endeavour Reef, Captain Cook was more than ever aware of the danger of coral reefs. On 5 June 1770 danger again apparently threatened the *Endeavour*; Joseph Banks, the great naturalist who accompanied Cook on the journey, wrote in his diary:

> At dinner time we were alarmd afresh by the usual report of a shoal just ahead: it provd however to be no more than a bank or regular layer of a Brownish colour extending itself upon the sea, which indeed had very much the appearance of a shoal while at a distance. It was formd by innumerable small atoms each scarce ½ a line in length yet when lookd at in a microscope consisting of 30 to 40 tubes, each hollow and divided throughout the whole length into many cells.

Oscillatoria erythraea (Sea Sawdust) forming streaks on the surface of the sea

Cook's seamen, who originally thought that the substance was the spawn of fish, eventually decided that this was not the case and called it Sea Sawdust.

Since Cook's time there have been numerous reports of this "mystery" phenomenon along the Queensland coast – variously termed "whale sperm", "whale food", "coral spawn" or "sea scum". The organism responsible is a Blue-green Alga, *Oscillatoria erythraea*. Individual filaments of the alga are in the vicinity of only .01 mm in diameter but usually fifty or more are loosely welded together into a small raft just visible to the naked eye as a sawdust-like fleck. These float to the surface, buoyed by small internal gas containers. There they are concentrated by wind into great rusty surface streaks, sometimes stretching for many kilometres.

If the alga accumulates on a shore it decays rapidly, turning verdigris green and giving off an offensive odour, sometimes likened to chlorine or iodine. Material trapped in pools soon gives up its red pigment to the water which looks as though someone might recently have washed a badly gashed foot there. Large accumulations along a shore may lead to the death of nearly all marine animals in the vicinity. This is probably due in part to depletion of dissolved oxygen by the rotting mass and in part to the release of a toxin which the alga is thought to contain. In Brazil, a recurring illness among coast dwellers, involving respiratory troubles, fever, muscular pains and rash, has been linked with appearances of *O. erythraea*. The symptoms apparently are induced by inhalation of minute droplets of the toxin in the atmosphere. Along the Great Barrier Reef there is a belief that coral scratches are more likely to turn septic when *O. erythraea* is in the water.

The occurrence of *Oscillatoria* "blooms" is a widespread phenomenon in tropical seas, and the Red Sea owes its name to occasional blooms of the alga. There has even been speculation that some references in the Bible to water or the sea being turned to blood may have some connection with blooms of this alga, for example, in *Rev.* 8:8," and the third part of the sea became blood".

Division Phaeophyta (Brown Algae)

Chnoospora implexa   Tangle Balls

During winter and early summer this is one of the most common algae on some reef flats. Its repeatedly forked, slightly flattened branches only about 1 mm in diameter are intricately tangled to form springy brown clumps sometimes 30 cm across. In its repeated forking it shows some resemblance to species of *Dictyota* but is easily distinguished by the only slight flattening of its branches.

Particularly in early summer the loosely attached clumps start to break away, and many of the "balls" are washed up onto the beach where they soon lose their springiness, collapsing into dark, rust-brown tangles.

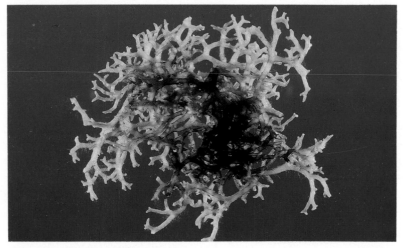

Chnoospora implexa (Tangle Balls)

Colpomenia sinuosa   Oyster Thief

Swimmers and anglers in southern Queensland are sometimes annoyed by concentrations of "wet cornflakes" in the surf. These brown flakes are fragments of *Colpomenia sinuosa* which, from time to time, is washed out from estuaries in considerable quantities and is quickly broken up by pounding waves. This is a widespread alga common on coral reefs as well as on temperate shores. It forms a brittle, yellow-brown, rounded or irregularly convoluted bladder several centimetres across. A second species, *C. peregrina*, is very similar but can often be distinguished by its more papery texture and more "bubbly" appearance. Entire bladders of the two species are often washed up in large quantities on beaches in early summer.

At one time, *Colpomenia* became a serious pest in oyster beds in France. Spores settled on the oysters, and as the plants increased in size and buoyancy many of the oysters were floated away. The loss was reduced by dragging spiny branches over the beds to tear and puncture the floats.

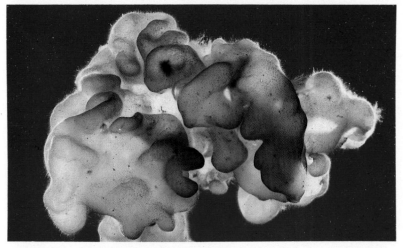

Colpomenia sinuosa (Oyster Thief)

Cystoseira trinodis   Chain Float

Chain Float is one of the tallest algae of the Reef, sometimes reaching to a metre in length. Resembling the Sargassums in general appearance, it is distinguished from them by having distinctly elongate floats often in chains of two or three. Leaves are restricted to the basal, densely warty part of the stem or are sometimes lacking altogether.

Cystoseira trinodis (Chain Float)

Dictyopteris australis

Plants reach 30 cm in length and have the form of a repeatedly forked, membranous ribbon about 1 cm broad. There is

Dictyopteris acrostichoides

some resemblance to species of *Dictyota* but *Dictyopteris australis* can be readily distinguished by the presence of a midrib. The ribbons are marked by numerous hair groups arranged in a series of inverted Vs.

Dictyopteris acrostichoides is similar to *D. australis*, but lacks the fine lateral veins of the latter species.

Dictyota bartayresii

Dictyota bartayresii is a repeatedly forked, membranous brown ribbon, the two branches of a pair developing evenly or unevenly. The larger plants, up to 30 cm long, stream out in the current as a cluster of ribbons but the smaller plants are often prostrate. Reproductive bodies appear as dark-brown specks scattered over the surface. When submerged, some plants show a delicate bluish iridescence.

Dictyota bartayresii

Ectocarpus mitchellae

Newly available surfaces permanently submerged in the shallow waters of the reef flat are often colonized first by a soft brown fur, a few millimetres to a few centimetres long, of *Ectocarpus mitchellae*, which some workers list as *Giffordia mitchellae*. Other species of *Ectocarpus* may mingle in this fur,

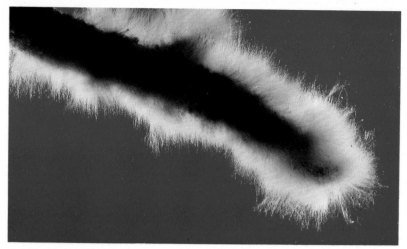

Ectocarpus mitchellae

and some form brownish wisps on larger algae. Most of the Brown Algae are comparatively large, robust and often of complex form; *Ectocarpus* is one of the few which are filamentous.

Hormophysa triquetra   Three-corners

This is a coarse alga up to about 30 cm high. The branches, up to 1 cm broad, are typically three-sided or with three prominent and irregularly toothed wings, although flattened

Hormophysa triquetra (Three-corners)

branches may occur also. In the upper, slender branches, small vesicles or floats often develop.

Hydroclathrus clathratus   Monkey Feathers, Wire-netting Alga

The scientific name, based on the Latin *clathratus* (latticed), doubly implies the net-like form of this distinctive alga. The rounded meshes are of variable size, up to 5 cm in diameter in fragile plants growing in calm water, but much smaller in the robust compact plants in more turbulent situations. Whole plants vary in size from 5 to 60 cm in diameter. They often become detached and are washed up on beaches in early summer when, with *Chnoospora implexa* and the two species of *Colpomenia*, they may form a thick brown mat somewhat lacking in eye and nose appeal.

The common name Monkey Feathers, which is of South-East Asian origin, does not give much clue to the plant's appearance but at least is easily remembered.

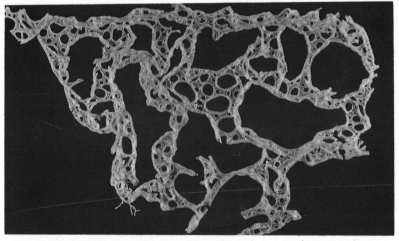

Hydroclathrus clathratus (Monkey Feathers)

Lobophora variegata

Lobophora variegata forms chocolate-brown to rust-brown leathery fans up to 10 cm across, marked by fine radial striations. These grow mainly prostrate and are often loosely attached at several points on their underside, becoming difficult to remove intact. In some places where they grow particularly vigorously they may encroach on the living branches of coral, sometimes killing them.

Lobophora variegata

Padina   Funnel Weed

One character in particular distinguishes *Padina* from other brown algae with fan-shaped fronds; this is the inrolled outer margin of the frond, easily detected by touch as a marginal ridge. The frond expands by a continuous unrolling process, while growth by the protected margins maintains the roll. In the water, *Padina* often looks like a cluster of delicate, pale-brown funnels up to about 6 cm across; but as soon as the funnels are removed from the water they spread out to reveal their undulate fan form. The chalky appearance of some fronds is caused by surface calcification which, among the Brown Algae, is unique to *Padina*.

Held up to the light the frond can be seen to be marked by fine, concentric curved lines, which are rows of microscopic hairs. When reproductive bodies are formed these also occur in lines, rather darker and broader than the hair lines. The relative position of hair and spore lines is a useful character in distinguishing species of *Padina*; *P. tenuis* has a hair line

Padina australis (Funnel Weed)

below each reproductive line while *P. australis* has a hair line on each side of a reproductive line.

Ralfsia expansa   Tar Spot

Dark-brown, almost black crusts on intertidal rocks and dead coral are usually plants of *Ralfsia expansa*. On a smooth surface the crust is typically round; as it increases in size the

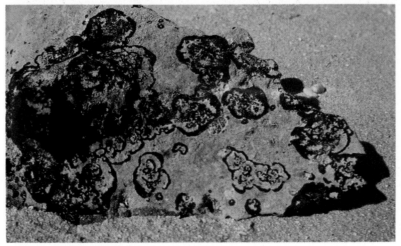

Ralfsia expansa (Tar Spot)

older, central parts die leaving a ring-shaped form. Over irregular, much-branched coral the colonies sometimes coalesce to form an almost complete crust over the protruding surfaces.

Sargassum   Sargassum

Among coral reef algae, species of *Sargassum* are relatively large plants mostly 20–100 cm long. The brown, leaf-like appendages borne along the stem give the specimens some resemblance to a flowering plant. In addition to the leaves, most specimens bear small floats, a few millimetres across, which help to hold the submerged plant erect. It is to these floats that the alga owes its name, *Sargassum* being derived from a Portuguese word for a small grape, which the floats were thought to resemble. Receptacles, the reproductive branches, occur in fertile specimens as clusters of fingers, cones or blades to about 1 cm long, often arising from the stalk of the leaf or bladder.

The fabled Sargasso Sea of the Atlantic Ocean is an area where plants, originally broken away from shores in the West Indies, are able to survive by virtue of the floats which keep them near the surface. There they live indefinitely, the decay of older parts releasing branches as growth proceeds at the tips. Although the amounts of algae present in the

Sargassum sp.

Sargasso Sea are large, there are not the impenetrable masses of some stories. Columbus, on his voyage of discovery to North America, used the presence of floating *Sargassum* to encourage his sailors to proceed further, claiming that it was a sign of approaching land.

About forty species have been recorded from Queensland but the group here is a poorly understood one and, at the present stage of knowledge, it is difficult to determine specimens with certainty. One species, common at Heron Island and easily recognized, is *S. polycystum*; it is unusual among species of *Sargassum* in having prostrate attaching branches, and very small leaves often no more than 1 mm wide and 1 cm long; the stem, particularly in the lower part, is very warty.

See also in chapter 6, "Flotsam".

Stypopodium flabelliforme

At first sight *Stypopodium flabelliforme*, with its fan-shaped fronds, up to 7 cm in diameter, marked by concentric hair lines, might easily be mistaken for a species of *Padina*. However, it differs clearly from members of that genus in lacking a rolled margin. The crisp, ruffled fronds are often linked to each other here and there to form a clump which shows a pale blue-green iridescence when submerged.

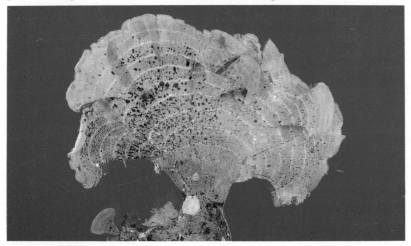

Stypopodium flabelliforme

Turbinaria ornata   Spiny Tops

Seaweeds in general are not harsh plants but *Turbinaria ornata* is one of the exceptions. The axis, up to 20 cm high, is closely beset with short, firm, top-shaped branches, each with a rigid spiny rim. Many of the "tops" develop an internal cavity which acts as buoy, holding the plant erect when submerged. Thus, the dome-shaped tips of *Turbinaria* plants are among the first algae to break the surface on a falling tide.

In spite of its unpromising appearance, Spiny Tops has been eaten in parts of South-East Asia. Green Turtles, which are vegetarian, have sometimes been found with considerable quantities of *Turbinaria* in their stomachs.

The name *Turbinaria* is applied also to some species of corals, a source of possible confusion in reading accounts of coral reefs.

Turbinaria ornata (Spiny Tops)

Division Rhodophyta (Red Algae)

Acanthophora spicifera

Although a Red Alga, *Acanthophora spicifera* is yellow-brown to olive green in colour. It grows as loose clumps, up to 15 cm high, of regularly branched, crisp and brittle stems about 1.5 mm in diameter, attached to the substrate at several points. The branches bear numerous stubby branchlets, 1–2 mm long, each with several spines. These short spiny branchlets enable *Acanthophora* to be distinguished from the better-known and somewhat similar Laurencias which have rounded ends to the branchlets.

Acanthophora spicifera

Amansia glomerata   Red Rosette

Crevices in the spur and groove system and the under-surfaces of coral clumps on the reef flat are the places to search for this Red Alga, one of the comparatively few non-calcified Reds on the Reef to show an obvious red colour. *Amansia glomerata* occurs in rosettes, 3–6 cm across, of radiating, ribbon-like, fringed branches; the branch apex looks cut off because of an inrolling of its edge.

Amansia glomerata (Red Rosette)

Amphiroa   Coral Weed

Amphiroa belongs to a group of calcified Red Algae whose high lime content makes them rigid and brittle, and occasionally leads to their being mistaken for corals. The plants form clumps of repeatedly forked rigid segments, with very narrow uncalcified joints at or near the forks, and so are placed among the articulated or jointed coralline Red Algae. These joints give the plants a degree of flexibility when living but once dry they become brittle and the plant readily fragments.

See also in chapter 6, "Flotsam".

Amphiroa crassa

This is a fairly robust plant, growing in clumps with a single point of attachment, usually in shaded crevices in the seaward platform or the spur and groove system. The dull pink branches are cylindrical or slightly flattened, up to 2 mm in diameter, rather irregularly branched with the joints sometimes a little above the point of forking.

Amphiroa crassa (Coral Weed)

Amphiroa foliacea

The more common species of *Amphiroa* on the reef, *A. foliacea* forms flattened clumps of regularly forked, flattened branches 1–2.5 mm in diameter; each clump has several points of attachment to the substrate. Although a mauve or pink colour when growing in a shaded position, it is a conspicuous orange-yellow when well illuminated.

Amphiroa foliacea (Coral Weed)

Asparagopsis taxiformis   Iodine Weed

Iodine Weed is a less than complimentary name for a beautiful alga restricted mainly to areas below low-water mark. A prostrate axis produces erect branches with many fine lateral branchlets forming a pale-pink plumose frond up to 15 cm high. The plant contains iodine vesicles, and it is these structures which are responsible for the distinctive and pungent odour of a shore on which *Asparagopsis taxiformis* has been washed up in quantity.

In 'Hawaii this alga is one of the most popular of the numerous species eaten there. After soaking in fresh water, salting and pounding, it is eaten in small quantity as a relish with other foods.

Asparagopsis taxiformis (Iodine Weed)

Ceratodictyon spongiosum   Sponge Weed

Anyone who took this structure to be a sponge would be half right. It is one of those strange, composite organisms made up of a plant and an animal living in close association, probably to their mutual advantage. The plant partner is the Red Alga *Ceratodictyon spongiosum* and, although this makes up the bulk of the body, its sponge partner has a strong influence on the combined form so that the general impression is sponge-like rather than plant-like. The irregular, rigid finger-like

Ceratodictyon spongiosum (Sponge Weed)

branches, dark green to dull purple, may be prostrate or may form erect clusters 10–15 cm high, often with fusions between parts which touch each other.

Chondrococcus hornemannii

This is one of the most decorative Red Algae of the Reef, forming bright pink, much-divided, fern-like fronds up to

Chondrococcus hornemannii

about 12 cm long. Main branches are 1–1.5 mm broad but diameter diminishes gradually towards the tips. Plants are found mainly on the reef rock rim and seaward platform.

Eucheuma denticulatum   Jelly Weed

Although not a common alga, *Eucheuma denticulatum* is a distinctive one in both appearance and texture. The branches, either prostrate or spreading away from the substrate, are 1.5–4 mm broad and at intervals carry whorls of conical spines. The plants are tough, very rubbery, and vary in colour from green through yellow-brown to red or purple. Small bouldery pools in the reef rock rim sometimes support this alga.

Eucheuma denticulatum (Jelly Weed)

Species of *Eucheuma* have been harvested from tropical and subtropical areas, particularly from South-East Asia, as a source of a gelatinous material resembling agar, and valued particularly as a thickening and stabilizing agent. Natural stands are unable to supply the demand, so *Eucheuma* culture is now undertaken in South-East Asia where it is grown on nets spread over reefs.

Galaxaura

Species of *Galaxaura* form pink, often loosely rounded clumps 10–20 cm high of repeatedly forked branches, usually cylindrical, but flattened in a few species. The branches are of fairly even diameter throughout and have slightly depressed tips. Although there is a firm outer layer, weakly calcified, the internal construction is of very loosely arranged filaments, allowing the branches to be easily crushed between finger and thumb. This is a useful field character, distinguishing species of *Galaxaura* from some species of *Amphiroa* to which they may bear a superficial resemblance. At least six species of *Galaxaura* occur in the area.

See also in chapter 6, "Flotsam".

Galaxaura oblongata

The cylindrical branches, 1–2 mm broad, are hairless throughout.

Galaxaura rugosa

Although showing considerable resemblance to *Galaxaura oblongata*, this species can be distinguished from it by the presence of hairs on the lower branches.

Galaxaura rugosa

Galaxaura subfruticulosa

The dull-red hairs which densely cover all the branches make this a distinctive, readily recognized species.

Galaxaura subfruticulosa

Gelidiella acerosa   Mermaid's Comb

Mermaid's Comb is not a conspicuous plant but is often one of the most common and most widespread plants of the Reef.

Gelidiella acerosa (Mermaid's Comb)

Frequently, several rigid, olive-fawn, arching branches arise from the attachment and bear comb-like teeth along one or both sides.

In India, this species is gathered for the extraction of agar but since the plants are seldom more than a few centimetres high and must be gathered by hand, it is economically valuable only where labour is cheap.

Gracilaria

Most species of *Gracilaria* have numerous cylindrical branches and a firm, sometimes cartilaginous texture. Although they belong to the Red Algae they rarely exhibit a distinct red or pink colour and are mostly found in various shades of yellow, green, olive or purple.

Species of *Gracilaria* yield agar, a material which, when heated in water and allowed to cool, sets to form a firm gel. A particularly important use for agar is in the preparation of media for growing microorganisms. Other uses are in the tinning of soft meats, such as camp pie, sheep's tongue and some fish, and in the preparation of confectionery and sauces. Japan has traditionally been a major source of agar, and when this supply was cut off during World War II, Australia, after some delay, was able to produce a satisfactory agar from *G. verrucosa* growing in inlets mainly along the coast of New South Wales. The species growing along the Great Barrier Reef are not present in quantities sufficient to have any commercial potential. In South-East Asia species of *Gracilaria* are eaten either raw or after boiling.

Gracilaria arcuata

This a low-growing, often mainly prostrate plant with rigid, pointed, often curved branches 1.5–4 mm wide.

Gracilaria crassa

The rigid branches up to 3 mm broad may be either prostrate or erect but seldom more than a few centimetres high. Characteristically, the branches have blunt apices.

Gracilaria arcuata

Gracilaria crassa

Gracilaria edulis   Ceylon Moss

This is the tallest of the three species noted here, reaching 20 cm in height. The repeated irregular forking of the erect branches produces parallel clusters of branches which, compared with the other species, are fairly pliant.

An alga somewhat similar in appearance to *Gracilaria edulis* is *Solieria robusta*, which reaches a length of 15–20 cm and is

Gracilaria edulis (Ceylon Moss)

distinctly red or pink in colour. It is several times branched from all sides, the cylindrical branches mostly 1–3 mm broad and tapered gradually to fine points. A distinctive feature is the sharp narrowing at the base of each branch.

Hypnea pannosa   Spine Weed

Spine Weed is a very variable alga, often forming crisp, brittle clumps which nestle among coral branches on the reef flat,

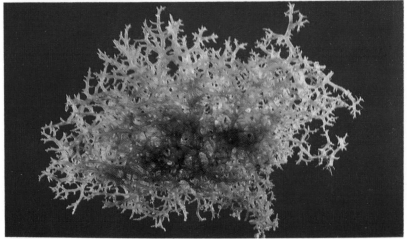

Hypnea pannosa (Spine Weed)

and ranging in colour from a pale blue-green through olive and purplish to fawn. It is much-branched with many short spine-like branches up to about 1 mm in diameter; branches often fuse when they touch each other.

Other species of *Hypnea* occur on the Reef and these also are characterized by the possession of numerous, short, spiny branches, in some cases more sharply marked off from the main branches than in *H. pannosa*.

Jania adhaerens

Jania adhaerens is one of the jointed or articulated coralline algae. Its very slender branches, well under a millimetre broad, are repeatedly branched and consist of a series of calcified segments and very short uncalcified joints, a detail possible to detect only with the aid of a lens.

Although not conspicuous there, it is a very common constituent of the algal turf covering the reef rock rim. It occurs more obviously as tufts 2–3 cm long attached to some of the larger algae.

Jania adhaerens

Laurencia   Club Weed

The species of Laurencia have much-branched stems carrying numerous stubby, cylindrical or club-shaped branchlets, each with a tuft of microscopic hairs protruding from the depressed apex. There are numerous species on the Reef, many of them small and difficult to identify.

Laurencia intricata

Although there is some variation in colour among plants of this species, most are distinctly green, making it difficult to believe that they are Red Algae, although a pinkish tinge in the ends of the branches of some specimens gives a clue to their relationship. *Laurencia intricata* is a common alga on the reef flat, forming crisp clumps up to 15 cm long, often attached to small pieces of rubble over the sandy floor. Its club-shaped branches are approximately 0.5 mm broad. In more turbulent situations it may form compact cushion-like clumps.

Laurencia intricata (Club Weed)

Laurencia majuscula

In general form this species is similar to *Laurencia intricata*, with which it often grows, but can be distinguished by its red-brown to yellow-brown colour and, when the two are seen together, by the rather finer branchlets of *L. majuscula*.

Laurencia majuscula (Club Weed)

Liagora valida

Liagora valida forms dense clumps, up to about 15 cm high, consisting of repeatedly forked branches 0.5–1 mm broad, often intricately tangled together. The clump feels harsh to the touch because of extensive calcification which cracks in many places so that the branches are fairly flexible. Calcifica-

Liagora valida

tion largely obscures the pink colour of the filaments which make up the plant so that the clump appears only very pale pink except for the deep-pink apices where calcification is lacking. Several other species of *Liagora* also occur on the Reef.

Lithophyllum kotschyanum

On the seaward platform, where coral is usually particularly well developed, there are often numerous colonies of a heavily calcified alga which at first sight might be mistaken for a coral. The pink, often bun-shaped colonies, up to 12 cm across, consist of closely placed forked branches, cylindrical or distinctly flattened, and often united in their lower part. Stony plants of this type were once thought to be animals, and were termed "nullipores" (animals without pores) to distinguish them from corals.

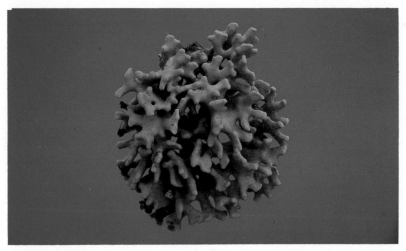

Lithophyllum kotschyanum

A similar species, *Lithophyllum moluccense*, is found mainly on the reef flat. Its branches taper towards the apices which are more or less sharp compared with those of *L. kotschyanum* which are always blunt.

Neogoniolithon fosliei

There are several species of heavily calcified Red Algae which form stony pink encrustations over dead coral, and are without surface excrescences other than those which reflect irregularities in the substrate below. Published information on this group of plants in the Reef area is meagre and many of the species are not easy to recognize in the field without considerable experience. *Neogoniolithon fosliei* is one of the more distinctive species because of the often bluish tinge in the pink crust and because of the unusually large size, 1 mm or more in diameter, of the shallowly conical conceptacles, or cavities, in which the spores are formed.

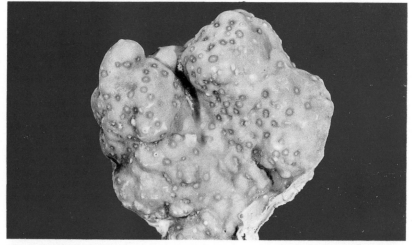

Neogoniolithon fosliei

Peyssonnelia

Species of *Peyssonnelia* form encrusting plants, rounded or irregular in outline, and vary in colour from red through yellow-pink to orange or orange-brown. Most are difficult to remove from the substrate. Although it is not obvious on superficial examination, there is always some calcification within or on the lower part of the crust. Most of the several species require microscopic examination for certain identification.

One common species is *P. conchicola* which is often found attached to loose pieces of coral or shells. It is usually bright

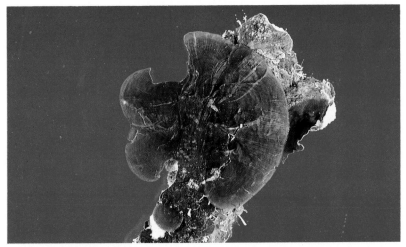

Peyssonnelia inamoena

red to yellow-pink in colour, and shows distinct radial striations.

On heavily shaded surfaces, *P. inamoena* is a common species, deep red in colour, in part encrusting but often with bracket-like extensions which are extremely brittle.

Plocamium hamatum   Hook Weed

This beautiful alga is restricted to the heavily shaded crevices and caverns in the spur and groove system of the reef. Roofs

Plocamium hamatum (Hook Weed)

of these cavities are often festooned with the deep red plants whose beauty is apparent only when brought out into the light. Flattened fronds, up to about 15 cm high, are much divided in a distinctive branching pattern with groups of three branches alternating along the axes. The *hamatum* part of the name is derived from the Latin *hamatus* (hooked), and refers to the fact that a few of the branches may grow into hooks or coils. It is likely that these hooks allow a detached fragment to catch on some obstruction, where it starts a new plant.

Trichogloea requienii

This beautiful alga is a characteristic inhabitant of pools on the reef rock rim and seaward platform. Its loosely tufted clumps of much-branched, tapering fronds are a soft pink or fawn in colour; branches may be up to 20 cm long and 2–5 mm broad, each with a chalky core visible through the translucent, coloured outer layers.

The plants are exceptionally soft and slimy to the touch. Because of this softness, they respond to any slight movement in the water much more than do most other algae, and almost give the impression of waving, like tentacles of a large anemone.

Trichogloea requienii

Yamadaella cenomyce

The rubble crest, the bouldery area near the outer edge of many reefs, is the place where *Yamadaella cenomyce* is often found in abundance. It forms mainly prostrate tufts, attached at several points, consisting of repeatedly forked branches, 0.5–1 mm in diameter, with the forks often widely diverging.

Yamadaella cenomyce

The heavy calcification consists of loosely arranged crystals, so the plant remains pliant. It is the calcification which is responsible for the mainly dirty-white colour of the plants, usually only the branch tips showing dull pink.

3   *The islands*

Coral cays

A cay is a tropical island, but not just any tropical island. It is a structure supported on a coral reef, sometimes standing only a few centimetres above high-water mark, and made up almost entirely of the remains of calcareous animals and plants which once inhabited the reef.

The material may be nearly all sand, or nearly all shingle and larger fragments, or a mixture of the two. In general, the sandy cays lie towards the western end of the supporting reef. This is because the waves driven by the prevailing south-east and north-east winds swing around each side of

Ridges of coarse coral rubble forming Fairfax Island, the parts beyond tidal influence stained dark grey by Blue-green Algae.

the reef and, where they meet near the western end, lose force and deposit the particles they carry in suspension. Eventually this accumulation may reach to above normal high-water mark, where wind takes over from water as the main agent moulding its form. Particularly along the south-eastern side, the prevailing wind may pile up marginal dune ridges a metre or more above the general level of the cay. On Wreck Island the ridge is unusually high, rising to about 5 m above the adjacent level, while on Tryon Island one knoll reaches to 9 m above reef-flat level.

In the few cases where the cay is near the eastern, or weather, side of a reef, it is usually rubbly, the larger, heavier fragments of which it is composed having been deposited by the violent waves that tore them from the nearby reef surface; the finer fragments were carried further, perhaps to form a sand cay near the western side of the same reef. On some rubble cays the concentric ridges of successively deposited material can be seen. Unlike the mobile particles of which sand cays are built, these rubble fragments are too heavy to be moved by wind and, except at the margins where they are wave pounded, stay where they were originally deposited, each ridge recording some past period of violent weather.

It is the sand cays rather than the rubble cays which generally attract visitors. Among the best-known sand cays of

Masthead Island, a sand cay in the southern part of the Great Barrier Reef Province.

Low Isles, a lighthouse cay in the central part of the Great Barrier Reef Province.

the Great Barrier Reef are Heron Island near the southern end of the Reef area and Green Island off Cairns. Both are cays of medium size. One of the largest is North West Island, about 1.8 km long, while the cays at Low Isles off Port Douglas and North Reef in the Capricorn Group, which carry lighthouses, are less than 200 m long.

Newly deposited sand is not left bare for long, and the process of plant colonization is much the same whether the

Thuarea involuta, an early colonizer of newly deposited sand

sand is part of a newly formed cay or a recent accumulation at the margin of an established one. Low-growing grasses and herbs are generally the first plants to appear. These pioneers, as is generally the lot of colonists, have to put up with difficult conditions. They grow in a substrate deficient in many nutrients and with a poor water-retaining capacity, they are subject to strong, salt-laden winds, and there is the ever-present danger of being buried or uncovered by the shifting of wind-blown sand. Nevertheless, some of these pioneers soon become established and partly stabilize the area. By catching wind-blown particles they often build up the level to a safer height above high-water mark, while decay of their older parts gradually leads to some enrichment of the sand.

So conditions gradually improve, and the way is prepared for the secondary pioneers, the shrubs and small trees, but even this community represents only a stage in the succession of the vegetation, and eventually these secondary pioneers are replaced by forest-forming species. Some cays have not passed beyond the grass/herb stage, others have reached the shrub stage, while many, such as Heron Island, have developed a central forest of *Pisonia grandis* or some species which represents the most advanced stage possible under existing conditions. On such islands, all three stages can be seen, the first two forming concentric bands round the central forest. So, although there may be local departures from the plan, in broad outline three zones of vegetation can be seen on many cays.

Grass and herb zone

This is the outermost zone, occupied by the initial colonizers, pushing its way seawards wherever opportunity offers, and losing ground as some combination of weather and tides erodes its outer margin. The common grasses of this zone are *Spinifex hirsutus*, *Sporobolus virginicus*, *Thuarea involuta* and *Lepturus repens*. Among the herbs are *Tribulus cistoides*, *Euphorbia atoto*, *E. tannensis*, *Cakile edentula*, *Canavalia rosea* and *Ipomoea pes-caprae* subsp. *brasiliensis*. Slight disturbance of the surface in this area often reveals a layer of sand, about 2 mm thick, stained slightly greenish by the presence of numerous minute colonies of the Blue-green Alga *Nostoc*

The pioneer grass and herb zone followed by the shrub zone on North West Island.

commune, one of the relatively few species of plants with the capacity to utilize atmospheric nitrogen. It is likely that this alga releases some nitrogenous products which become available to the pioneer flowering plants in this nutrient-impoverished sand.

Shrub zone

The plants of this zone form the marginal wind buffer, and are tolerant of the strong winds, sand-blasting and salt spray to which they are subjected from time to time. *Casuarina equisetifolia* var. *incana* with its weeping branchlets is usually the largest of these pioneers, but much more effective as wind breaks are the shrubby species such as *Argusia argentea* and *Scaevola sericea*. Accompanying these species are several others such as *Pandanus* spp., *Cordia subcordata*, *Suriana maritima*, *Abutilon albescens* and *Wedelia biflora*.

On some cays, Green and Loggerhead Turtles nest during summer in large numbers in both the grass and herb zone and the shrub zone, sometimes leaving the area looking as though bulldozed, with turtle tracks criss-crossing the churned surface. Brittle shrubs such as *Scaevola sericea* often suffer greatly in this invasion, a large proportion of their stems being destroyed. This annual churning probably impedes the advance of the shrub zone into the grass and herb zone, and may be responsible for the absence or poor development of *Scaevola sericea* along some stretches of shore.

Forest zone

Several tree species may occur here, the constituents varying in different parts of the Reef. On northern cays there is often a mixed forest with species such as *Diospyros ferrea* and *Planchonella obovata* as important constituents, the forest in some cases approximating to rainforest. However, the most distinctive forest is the one found on most cays of the Capricorn and Bunker Groups, where *Pisonia grandis* is the dominant species. This fine species reaches to a maximum height of 20 m, although on the windward side of the cay the trees are often wind-sheared and much lower, sometimes only a metre or so high. It is usually the tallest Pisonia on the cay which supports the great nest of the White-breasted Sea Eagle.

There is no other forest which quite resembles a Pisonia forest, with its massive smooth trunks, pale grey or cream except sometimes for a black sock at the base where Blue-green Algae have colonized the bark. The shade cast by the

Pisonia forest with burrows of Wedge-tailed Shearwaters

Pisonia canopy is, in some places, so dense that nearly all other plants are excluded, leaving the sand floor bare and making obvious the entrances to the numerous nesting burrows of the Wedge-tailed Shearwaters (*Puffinus pacificus*), popularly known as mutton birds. Here, with each step, one walks at risk of collapsing knee-deep into a cavity beneath. Such areas obviously should be avoided in the nesting season.

In the open glades within the Pisonia forest there are small trees and shrubs of a few other species such as *Ficus opposita*, *Pipturus argenteus* and *Celtis paniculata*. Interlaced scrambling stems of *Wedelia biflora* are likely to make passage difficult, and the marginal Pisonia trees enclosing the glade may be festooned by the white-flowered creeper *Ipomoea macrantha*.

The tendency always is for each zone of vegetation to push out into the younger one which has made the environment suitable for it and, in a sense, by doing so has prepared the way for its own destruction. As the Pisonia forest advances into the shrub zone, species such as *Casuarina equisetifolia* var. *incana* persist for a time, but no replacement seedlings can survive in the shade of the Pisonia canopy. Evidence of this invasion can be seen in some places in the Pisonia forest where decaying logs of *Casuarina*, in positions no longer capable of supporting this species, indicate the site of a former strand forest.

Within the Pisonia forest on some cays are scattered lumps of rock made up of cay material and brought to the surface as the roots of falling Pisonias levered them from the ground. Phosphates in the rain of excreta from the Black Noddies (*Anous minutus*) nesting in the branches above are dissolved under the acid conditions prevailing in the thick, dark humus layer often accumulating under the trees. These phosphates seep downwards until they reach the sandy, alkaline layer beneath where they precipitate out, cementing the sand to form a soft rock. On some cays, this so-called hard pan forms a layer 10–20 cm thick situated at a depth of about 30 cm.

In one sense, cays along the Queensland coast are desert isles, since most of them are waterless and the small pools which occur on a few supply only brackish water. But these isles have such charm that having once visited such a place one lives in hope of returning.

Continental islands

In addition to the cays there are numerous other islands, the continental islands, which are essentially detached pieces of the mainland. The shores of these islands often present a series of rocky headlands interspersed with sandy beaches. Such islands provide a more varied plant habitat than do the cays, and generally support a more varied flora resembling that on the adjacent mainland. While they are not as intimately connected with the Reef as are the cays, which owe their existence to the remains of innumerable reef organisms, many of them have associated fringing coral reefs and are places of great beauty and interest.

Part of Brampton Island, one of the continental islands.

4 *Plants of the shore*

It is the flowering plants, with a single representative of the pines, which make up the conspicuous terrestrial vegetation of the shores of coral reef areas. The arrangement of flowering plants into families used here is the one adopted in *Flora of Australia* (1981–) and proposed by A. Cronquist.[1]

1. A. Cronquist (1981), An integrated system of classification of flowering plants (New York: Columbia University Press).

Family Aizoaceae

Sesuvium portulacastrum　　　　　　　　　Sea Purslane

Sea Purslane is a succulent sprawling plant particularly common in wet saline areas, but occurring also on sand dunes. The prostrate or semiprostrate stems are often reddish or orange-red, and bear shiny strap-shaped opposite leaves which are too fleshy for the veins to be distinguished. Pink, five-petalled star-like flowers are borne singly on fairly short stalks.

This is one of several fleshy salt-marsh plants which make a reasonable green vegetable after light boiling.

Sesuvium portulacastrum (Sea Purslane)

Tetragonia tetragonioides　　　　　New Zealand Spinach

Although it is usually known here as New Zealand Spinach, this plant is a native of Australia as well, being wide spread along the Pacific shores. Often sprawling in habit, it has thick but rather brittle stems and diamond-shaped leaves of unusual texture; the bulging surface cells give a glistening effect and make the leaves somewhat clammy to the touch. The flowers are relatively inconspicuous, yellow, and borne

Tetragonia tetragonioides (New Zealand Spinach)

singly or in pairs almost concealed in the leaf axils; they are followed by fleshy horned fruits.

Shoots of this species are edible as a cooked green vegetable, one of the best of the native plants for this purpose.

Family Amaranthaceae

Achyranthes aspera   Chaff Flower

A coarse herb, sometimes almost a shrub, *Achyranthes* has opposite, hairy, elliptical leaves produced at swollen nodes on square stems. Successive pairs of leaves are at right angles to one another and the branches in their axils develop equally to produce a symmetrical appearance.

The flowers are crowded in silvery-lavender spikes, sometimes 20 cm or more in length, with a somewhat scaly appearance; this is responsible for the botanical name derived from the Greek *achyron* (chaff) and *anthos* (flower). The "chaff" consists of small pinkish bracts which conceal the true flowers. Buds near the apex of the spike are directed upwards, and bend outwards as they mature; then, as the fruits develop, they turn downwards so that they lie almost parallel

Achyranthes aspera
(Chaff Flower)

to the axis. The spikes appear spiny but are no more than rough to the touch.

Although there is no record of Australian Aborigines using the plant medicinally, it has been used in other countries against a surprisingly wide variety of ailments including tetanus, dropsy, snake-bite, dysentery and hydrophobia, making it almost a complete medicine chest. The leaves have been cooked and eaten as a green vegetable in some areas.

Family Apiaceae (Umbelliferae)

Trachymene sp.

On some of the cays an early colonizer of sand or coral rubble is this member of the carrot family. It grows as a compact, almost cushion-like rosette of much-divided leaves. The

Trachymene sp.

Trachymene sp.

numerous button-like clusters of minute white flowers are followed by tightly packed balls of flat, two-lobed fruits, green at first but finally a rusty brown. As the fruits are formed the stem elongates so a heavy crop is often the most conspicuous feature of the plant.

Family Apocynaceae

Alyxia spicata   Climbing Chain Fruit

Alyxia spicata is a woody vine which is inclined to straggle over the ground, acting as a trip wire for unwary bushwalkers; when support is available it is a twiner, one of the few in Queensland to twine in a clockwise direction. Distinctive features of the plant are the occurrence of the elliptical leaves in whorls of three to four and the flow of milky latex on injury. The small cream flowers, like minute Frangipani flowers, are in clusters in the leaf axils and are followed by unusual fleshy fruits consisting of two to four globose, black segments joined in a chain by very narrow necks.

Alyxia spicata (Climbing Chain Fruit)

Catharanthus roseus   Pink Periwinkle,
(Vinca rosea)   Madagascar Periwinkle

Originally grown as a garden ornamental, Pink Periwinkle is a hardy plant which has become widely naturalized in many parts of coastal Queensland and on a number of Reef islands. It is a herb with elliptical opposite leaves; symmetrical, pink

Catharanthus roseus (Pink Periwinkle, Madagascar Periwinkle)

or white five-petalled flowers have a narrow tube and flat "face". All parts of the plant exude a white latex when broken; they have a rather unpleasant rank odour.

This modest-looking plant is of great importance in medicine. Popular fifty years ago in treatment of diabetes, this has been eclipsed today by its use as a source of major drugs used in cancer chemotherapy.

Cerbera manghas   Dog Bane

An unattractive common name disguises a handsome small tree growing close to the shore, sometimes just within the limits of particularly high tides. In many ways this milky-sapped tree is reminiscent of the garden Frangipani, although the leafy branches are not as thick and fleshy. The handsome white flowers, up to 7 cm across, are borne in sprays at the ends of branches. Five asymmetric petals are widely spread as a flat plate with a small, sharply defined red centre fringed with hairs. The fragrance of the flowers is partly spoiled by a slightly unpleasant undertone. Fruits about 8 cm long hang like small green mangoes, and even when green are surprisingly light; some develop a rosy hue, mainly after falling.

The plant contains several poisonous glycosides, and in India the green fruits have been used for poisoning dogs, so

Cerbera manghas (Dog Bane)

giving rise to the common name. Violent vomiting and purging are reported to follow eating the small, oily kernel.

See also in chapter 6, "Flotsam".

Ochrosia elliptica   Blood Horn

Strikingly handsome, paired fruits, like a set of stout, cherry-red horns, draw immediate attention to this small tree. As the

Ochrosia elliptica (Blood Horn)

young fruits develop, the two members of a pair diverge further and further from each other so that finally they point in opposite directions. Each is almond-shaped and about 6 cm long. The red skin encloses a poisonous, white pith in which is embedded a bony, flattened, spindle-shaped stone.

The glossy leaves are mostly in whorls of four and are elliptical to elliptical-obovate, generally 8–15 cm long. Numerous fine, parallel veins depart from the midrib. A copious flow of milky latex follows injury to bark or leaves, and, on some skins, this may produce a burn-like weal.

The bark has been used to treat malaria but analysis has not revealed the presence of quinine.

Trees are usually found close to the sea, either bordering sandy or rocky shores or along the landward margins of mangrove forests.

Family Araliaceae

Schefflera actinophylla   Umbrella Tree

Handsome and distinctive, the Umbrella Tree has been taken into cultivation far south of its natural habitat in tropical Queensland and, as its fruits are attractive to birds which distribute the seeds, it has become naturalized in some subtropical areas. It has also been popular as an indoor potplant in overseas countries.

Schefflera actinophylla (Umbrella Tree)

The tree is stout, often with several thick branches from near the base, but not particularly tall, about 12–15 m. Palmately compound leaves have up to sixteen glossy, stalked leaflets radiating from the apex of a common stalk; at the broad base of this are two stipules which clasp the stem, and a large scar is left when the leaf falls. Numerous dense heads of small flowers, little more than 1 cm across, are carried on stiff radiating spokes above the foliage; both flowers and spokes are a deep red, making a fine display against a blue sky. The numerous small fleshy fruits which follow are also red and are a magnet for fruit-eating birds, as the flowers are for nectar-seekers.

Family Araucariaceae

Araucaria cunninghamii   Hoop Pine

The Whitsunday group of islands is one of the most scenic areas of coastal Queensland, and owes much of its distinctive beauty to the Hoop Pine which dominates so many of the rocky promontories. The tree is by no means restricted to such areas and, in fact, is a common rainforest species widely distributed in eastern Australia. As a pine tree, it has cones rather than flowers and fruits.

The distinct central trunk which persists throughout the life of the tree bears whorls of lateral branches from about half a metre to occasionally four metres apart, and directed either horizontally or slightly upwards or downwards. Branchlets are clothed with narrow, rigid, incurved, overlapping leaves, and it is the whole branchlet rather than the in-

Araucaria cunninghamii
(Hoop Pine)

dividual leaves which is eventually shed. In juvenile plants and on heavily shaded branches the leaves are dagger-shaped and arranged in two ranks. The prickly, elliptical female cones, roughly orange-sized, break up on the tree, and the broad seed units are dispersed by wind.

Plants on rocky headlands are often relatively stunted compared with specimens growing in more favourable situations where they may reach a height of approximately 53 m. The timber has been a particularly valuable one but most of the natural stands have now been cut.

Once the trunk of a Hoop Pine is on the ground the soft wood decays rapidly, but the bark is more resistant and after a few years may remain as a row of short cylinders or hoops from which the common name originates.

Family Arecaceae (Palmae)

Arenga australasica

Although Coconuts are the palm trees commonly seen on reef islands and tropical shores, there is a native palm common on Green Island. This is a species of *Arenga*, a genus important in South-East Asia as a source of sugar. *A. australasica* has pinnate leaves, as does the Coconut, 3–5 m in length and with a distinctly pale undersurface. The palms usually occur in groups, apparently due to branching just below ground level. There is a large amount of fibre associated with the sheathing leaf bases; in some South-East Asian species of *Arenga* such fibre has been used for thatching.

Cocos nucifera   Coconut

Probably no palm in the world is as well known as the Coconut, an essential backdrop, both in imagination and in fact, to the white tropical beach fringing the blue waters of a lagoon. Now a characteristic feature of many tropical Queensland shores, the Coconut was absent when Captain Cook sailed along the coast in 1770, and owes its presence

Cocos nucifera (Coconut)

here to people rather than to the ability of its fruit to float across oceans.

These beautiful palms, often with a yellowish tinge in the crown of shiny pinnate leaves, nearly always lean seawards giving slight assistance to those agile enough to climb for the nuts.

Although now widely distributed in tropical regions, the Coconut probably originated in the Indo-Malaysian region, where it has been one of the staffs of life, providing food, drink, lighting oil, fuel, fibre thatch and even building timber, although of a poor quality.

Although the derivation of the name *Cocos* is uncertain, the most common explanation is that the sailors of Vasco da Gama's voyage to India used for the fruit the Portuguese word *coco*, meaning ape, because the three holes in the husked shell gave it the appearance of an ape's face.

See also in chapter 6, "Flotsam".

Family Asclepiadaceae

Dischidia nummularia   Button Plant

An unusual epiphyte mainly growing on *Melaleuca viridiflora* (Broad-leaved Tea-tree) close to the sea, Button Plant is a milky-sapped creeping plant rooting at intervals in the paper bark of its support and sometimes hanging in strands like a necklace. Its opposite, fleshy leaves, rounded with a shortly pointed apex, are covered with a mealy, waxy layer giving them a greyish colour which blends with the pale bark of their background. Beneath the waxy layer the leaves are pale yellow-green. Small cream flowers are borne in groups on short stalks in the leaf axils. Some species of *Dischidia* harbour ants in specialized hollow leaves, but this association has not developed in *D. nummularia*.

Dischidia nummularia
(Button Plant)

Sarcostemma australe   Caustic Vine, Caustic Bush

When the leafless, cylindrical, grey-green stems of this plant scramble over trees and shrubs and hang in a tangled curtain, it is known as Caustic Vine. Sometimes however, as Caustic Bush, it grows as a self-supporting shrub. The smooth stems with opposite branches bear short clusters of white star-like flowers at the joints of the branches. All parts of the plant, if

Sarcostemma australe (Caustic Vine, Caustic Bush)

broken, will exude a milky latex which can be irritating to some skins, but which was used by Aborigines and early settlers as a dressing for wounds and ulcers. The plant has a reputation as a stock poison in Queensland and New South Wales.

Family Asteraceae (Compositae)

Bidens pilosa   Cobbler's Peg

Visitors to the shores and islands of north Queensland may be favourably impressed by a large herb with white daisy flowers about 4 cm across. They are less attracted to it when they recognize the plant as Cobbler's Peg, a very common weed throughout the tropics. In cooler areas the flower head is usually an inconspicuous cluster, not more than 1 cm across, of minute yellow tubular florets, but in the north the presence of five or six white wedge-shaped ray florets transforms it into a reasonably attractive daisy.

The flower head is followed by a cluster of thirty or so narrow dry fruits each with two or three barbed hooks at the apex, admirably adapted for animal dispersal. Pairs of coarsely toothed, simple or compound leaves are rich in tannin and have been used to prepare a diarrhoea treatment. This plant is one which in theory is edible, but in practice is unpalatable.

Bidens pilosa (Cobbler's Peg)

Wedelia biflora   Beach Sunflower

In the strand vegetation the Beach Sunflower is one of the commonest plants, its sprawling, straggling, arching canes

Wedelia biflora (Beach Sunflower)

sometimes forming dense thickets a metre or more high, and no pleasure to traverse. The opposite leaves with notched margins are somewhat harsh to the touch because of their stiff but inconspicuous hairs; when bruised, the leaves have an odour slightly reminiscent of crushed mango leaves. The yellow "flower", actually a head of small florets giving the impression of a single flower, resembles that of the Sunflower, although considerably smaller.

The rust fungus *Uromyces wedeliae* sometimes attacks the plant producing small dark-brown pustules of spores over the leaf surface.

In Tonga the plant has been used medicinally, the juice extracted by pounding the leaves between hot stones and then applied to wounds.

Family Bixaceae

Cochlospermum gillivraei   Native Kapok

Although Native Kapok is widespread in inland districts, it also forms a striking feature of some bouldery granite headlands such as occur at Bowen and Magnetic Island. The trees flower in spring and are spectacular, with their large yellow flowers, about 8 cm across, borne on leafless branches. Petals are deeply notched at their apices but the notch is concealed by the folding together of the two lobes. There are numerous red stamens, diminishing in size inwards, and a single style gradually broadening upwards, and with a minute, star-shaped orifice at its apex. Leaves appear later and are deeply divided into five to seven lobes. The fruit, obovate and about 8 cm long, contains numerous seeds and large quantities of fine fibres.

The bark has been used as a source of fibre by the Aborigines.

Cochlospermum gillivraei (Native Kapok)

Family Boraginaceae

Argusia argentea
(Tournefortia argentea,
Messerschmidia argentea)

Octopus Bush

No species is more characteristic of the strand than this striking silvery shrub. Young specimens direct to the sea a dense

Argusia argentea (Octopus Bush) – female inflorescence with flowers and
fruits

Argusia argentea (Octopus Bush) – an early colonizer presenting a dense
wall of foliage to the wind

wall of foliage right from sand level, and one has only to camp behind such a shelter on a windy day to appreciate what an effective shield it makes. Older specimens show a crooked branch system on a disproportionately massive trunk, giving them a form reminiscent of the dwarfed bonsai plants of Japan.

The rather brittle, slightly fleshy leaves are clothed with closely appressed white hairs which impart a distinctive silvery-grey appearance to the shrub. Upcurving of the leaf

Argusia argentea (Octopus Bush) – male flowers

Argusia argentea (Octopus Bush) – antler-like dead branches

margins and a reasonable rigidity allow the leaf to be used as a makeshift spoon. When the leaves fall, they leave broadly heart-shaped scars on the rather thick twigs. Dark-brown powdery pustules on the older leaves are spore masses of the rust fungus *Uromyces tairae*.

The flowering cluster close to the apex of a branch is surrounded by two to four leafy branches arising nearby and when the fruiting stalk finally falls its scar is surrounded by this group of diverging branches. In many cases only one of these eventually survives, so that at each point of original branching there is a bend in the stem. These accumulated bends result in the contorted or irregularly zigzag course so characteristic of branches in older specimens; they also give dead branches a curious antler-like form.

In the early stage of the inflorescence there is a close branch system with numerous small buds like a diminutive cauliflower; each of the several main branches forks up to three times. Final branches are at first tightly coiled downwards but as they gradually develop and uncoil the small squat flowers open in a double row on the upper side. Male and female flowers are borne on different plants. In male flowers the five well-developed anthers give fresh specimens a pale yellowish centre. Female flowers have only rudimentary brown anthers but the well-developed ovary is green, giving the flower a greenish centre.

As branches bearing male flowers uncoil, they come to stand erect with the clustered rows of spent flowers facing each other. Female branches, on the other hand, spread outwards and, with their double rows of crowded yellow-green fruits, bear a fancied resemblance to the undersurface of outstretched octopus arms.

Young leaves are edible either raw or boiled but their hairiness makes them unattractive as a vegetable, and they seem never to have been an important item of food. In some areas the dried leaves have been used as a tobacco substitute, and Pacific peoples have found various medicinal uses for the leaves; in New Caledonia they have been used against illness caused by eating toxic fish, and to relieve itching; in the Gilbert Islands juice extracted from the leaves has been used to reduce fever – three leaves for a child, nine for an adult; and in Fiji the plant was believed to be effective against various stomach troubles.

Cordia subcordata   Sea Trumpet

Seen against the blue of the sea, the bright orange flowers of
Cordia subcordata are among the most beautiful to be found
on a coral cay. As the cylindrical bud develops, the folded
petals protrude as an orange tip and finally expand to form a
trumpet-shaped flower about 4 cm across, with usually six
crinkled petals.

Cordia subcordata (Sea Trumpet)

The fruit is enclosed within the old calyx which forms a
narrow three-toothed crown. At maturity the fruit is ovate-
conical, 1–2 cm broad, and is surprisingly light because of its
corky outer layer which allows it to be dispersed readily by
water. Within the corky layer is a hard shell with four small
cavities each of which may contain a single seed about the
size of an apple seed. These are edible but hardly worth the
trouble of extraction. Seedlings are easily recognized by the
characteristic form of the first pair of leaves – each leaf a
broad wedge, prominently corrugate, and with irregularly
scalloped margins.

The tree is a small spreading one which at first sight might
be mistaken for *Pisonia grandis*. However it can be readily
distinguished from the latter by having only three to five
main lateral veins on each side of the midrib (usually seven to
twelve in *P. grandis*) and in the leaf blade being symmetrical
where it joins the leaf stalk.

Trunks do not reach sufficient size to be of any commercial use in Australia, but the wood is soft and durable and, in some Pacific islands, has been used for cups, dishes, canoes and fishing floats. In Fiji it was formerly used for making fire by friction. Both the leaves and scrapings of young stems from which the bark has been removed have been used in the Pacific area to prepare a medicine believed to cure diarrhoea.

Family Brassicaceae (Cruciferae)

Cakile edentula   Sea Rocket

Sea Rocket is an annual strand plant which forms spreading or rounded clumps to about 40 cm high. Its succulent leaves bear coarse, blunt, irregular teeth, the size of the leaves and the degree of indentation varying considerably in different parts of the plant. Stems are often distinctly purple.

Cakile edentula (Sea Rocket)

The small, pale mauve flowers, only about 5 mm across, have four petals arranged in a cross, and six stamens. This cross-like arrangement of the petals in members of the family is responsible for the name Cruciferae by which the family has commonly been known. As the fruit develops it takes on an unusual form, consisting of two one-seeded swollen cells, one above the other. The larger, upper one is more or less almond-shaped and tapers to a point; however, in many cases the lower segment fails to develop its seed, and remains as a small stalk. Once dry, the upper cell breaks off at a touch and may be dispersed by wind or by water. The lower cell remains firmly attached to the parent plant.

Family Cactaceae

Opuntia stricta   Prickly Pear

In 1927 two naturalists found a single plant of Prickly Pear growing on Masthead Island in the Capricorn Group. They pulled it up and threw it into the sea, but unfortunately this action was of no avail as this pest is now firmly established on Masthead Island and in several places forms impenetrable thickets several metres across.

Prickly Pear was introduced into Australia originally as a curiosity; the story of its spread 'n the 1920s to infest 27,000,000 hectares of country, mainly in Queensland, is well known, as is the story of its eventual control by its natural enemy, the larva of the *Cactoblastus* moth. Specimens near the sea shore are not so readily controlled by *Cactoblastus* as are those further inland.

Opuntia stricta (Prickly Pear)

Opuntia may have reached the islands by sea; the green pads are very resistant and are sometimes seen washed up on the beaches. It is possible also that it was introduced by birds which ate the succulent fruits in one place and evacuated the seeds in another.

The green pads are stems carrying out the functions of leaves, which are much reduced and disappear early. These stems are beset with modified shoots occurring as bundles of sharp spines and irritating barbed bristles. In earlier days the hard spines were used as substitute gramophone needles.

The purple-red fruits are edible, but care should be taken first to remove the bristles.

Family Caesalpiniaceae

Caesalpinia bonduc   Nicker Nut, Wait-a-while

This robust scrambler is a handsome plant with large bipinnate leaves up to 70 cm long. Leaves have about nine pairs of pinnae, each with ten or so pairs of leaflets; there is a pair of hooked prickles at the base of each pair of leaflets, more on the leaf axis at the base of the pinnae, with others scattered, so the plant is certainly not one that becomes more attractive on closer acquaintance.

Caesalpinia bonduc (Nicker Nut, Wait-a-while)

Sprays of yellow *Cassia*-like flowers are followed by broad pods about 6 cm long, closely covered with sharp straight prickles. On drying, the pods split along the upper side and part of the lower, remaining on the plant as a more or less heart-shaped dish with one or two seeds seated loosely inside. The seeds are marble-like, slightly flattened or angular, with a stony blue-grey seedcoat and a round brown spot on one side where the seed was attached in the pod.

The stout, hooked prickles on the stem and leaf axis are the obvious origin of the name Wait-a-while. These and the very rampant growth make thickets of the plant almost impenetrable.

An infusion of the leaves has in some countries been administered to eradicate worms, while the bitter seeds have been used as a tonic.

See also in chapter 6, "Flotsam".

Intsia bijuga   Queensland Teak,
                                          Johnstone River Teak

A deciduous rainforest tree which has some similarities to Indian Beech (*Pongamia pinnata*) and which sometimes is found growing along the shore is the Queensland Teak or Johnstone River Teak. The compound leaves of this species have one or two pairs of leaflets, with no terminal leaflet; the

Intsia bijuga (Queensland Teak, Johnstone River Teak)

leaflets are curved forwards and slightly overlap the ones behind. Terminal sprays of flowers, each with a single, large pink petal, are distinctive; the pod is about 15–20 cm long and contains several flattened dark-brown seeds loosely covered with a reddish-brown "fuzz".

See also chapter 6, "Flotsam".

Family Casuarinaceae

Casuarina equisetifolia var. *incana*   Coastal Sheoak

Sheoaks are usually the first trees to appear during dune colonization, and are characteristic of the strand flora of coral cays as well as of the mainland. The beautiful trees fringe the cay casting a dappled shade on the carpet of "needles" below,

Casuarina equisetifolia var. *incana* (Coastal Sheoak)

Casuarina equisetifolia var. *incana* (Coastal Sheoak) — branch with cones

Casuarina equisetifolia var. *incana* (Coastal Sheoak) – female inflorescences with protruding red stigmas

Casuarina equisetifolia var. *incana* (Coastal Sheoak) – male inflorescences with each stamen representing a single flower.

and a view of white beach and blue-green reef framed in a fringe of *Casuarina* is surely the epitome of the tropical island paradise.

Wind blowing through a grove of the trees may produce a sighing sound, and it has been suggested that "she" in Sheoak is an attempt to reproduce this sound in a common name. The true origin of the name is less romantic. Early settlers noted the similarity between the timber of English oak, with its broad deep medullary rays, and that of the Casuarinas. "She" was simply an old bushman's prefix denoting inferiority. The name *Casuarina* was given because of the supposed resemblance of the fine soft foliage to the plumage of the Cassowary (*Casuarius*), a large flightless bird of northern rainforests.

What are generally assumed to be leaves on a *Casuarina* are slender pendulous branchlets. These are unlike most branches in having no further branching and in having limited growth and life; they never reach more than about 30 cm in length and after several months are shed as leaves are. In fact, they have taken on the main function of leaves which, in this case, are reduced to minute, seven-toothed whorls of scales which occur along the branchlets, giving them a jointed appearance.

Young branchlets have a pale-grey appearance due to a layer of fine, woolly hairs. As the branchlets age, these hairs are shed except along seven fine longitudinal grooves. It is these hairs which are responsible for the overall greyish appearance of the Coastal Sheoak as compared with other Casuarinas.

During spring, the ends of new branchlets become slightly swollen, and here the whorls of scales are so close that they overlap one another. In these slender cone-like tips the male flowers are borne, seven in each whorl, each flower consisting of a single stamen which pushes out beyond the scales. Female flowers are borne on the same tree, also at the ends of branchlets which, in this case, are short, club-shaped structures only about 1 cm long. Two slender red stigmas from each flower, protruding beyond the scales, are the only parts of the female flowers visible. After fertilization the leaf scales, together with two small bracts surrounding each flower, increase in size and become fused to form the nobbly, woody cone. As the cone dries, the paired bracts separate, leaving numerous slits from each of which a small winged nut escapes.

As sheoaks are the trees usually nearest the high-tide level, they are often subject to erosion with changes in the beach. Washing away of the sand exposes the roots which frequently bear gall-like structures up to the size of a fist. These are masses of closely branched, specialized roots inhabited by a filamentous bacterium. This partnership has the ability to convert atmospheric nitrogen to a combined form usable by the green plant, an ability not possessed by higher plants without such partners. This unusual capacity probably plays an important part in enabling these trees to succeed in the infertile sand. Thus, Casuarinas are important in both stabilizing and enriching the soil and so preparing the way for other species incapable of colonizing the bare sand.

Two other species of *Casuarina* may be seen close to the shore. One is *C. glauca* (Swamp Oak, Swamp Sheoak), mainly restricted to low-lying swampy areas, and often with crooked branching. The other is *C. littoralis* (Black Sheoak) often with a neat conical form, at least in the early stages; the male and female flowers in this species are borne on different trees, and in spring the male specimens are sometimes so densely covered with the minute flowers that the whole tree takes on a rusty appearance.

See also in chapter 6, "Flotsam".

Family Chenopodiaceae

Salsola kali   Roly-poly

Roly-poly is an annual plant occurring from inland plains to sandy beaches; possibly more than one species is involved in this widespread population. Leaves are fleshy, more or less semicircular in section, 1–5 cm long, and in beach plants are often tinged with red or purple. They end in a short needle point which makes the plant difficult to handle. Specimens are branched from close to the base, and though at first more or less conical eventually may be almost globose, so that when dry and broken away from the root they are bowled along by the wind, scattering their seeds as they go, and often accumulating in great numbers against obstructions such as fences.

Salsola kali (Roly-poly)

Sarcocornia quinqueflora   Samphire,
(Salicornia australis)   Chicken Claws

One of the commonest plants of the salt flats is Samphire, a
low, shrubby succulent. The plant has a number of semiprostrate branches from which arise erect branched shoots to
15 cm or more high; older specimens may be woody at the
base. Stems are leafless, fleshy and jointed; they vary from
green to red or purple, the overall effect usually being
reddish. Minute flowers are produced, sunken at the joints of
slightly thickened branches.

Samphire is edible, raw or cooked, but has a high salt
content. European species were used as a source of soda for
making soap and glass, and are sometimes known as
Glasswort.

Occupying habitats similar to those of *Sarcocornia
quinqueflora*, and with a similar general appearance, are three
species of the genus *Halosarcia*, also commonly known as
Samphire. These may be distinguished by having only one
stamen in each of the minute flowers, *Sarcocornia* having
two.

Sarcocornia quinqueflora (Samphire, Chicken Claws)

Suaeda australis   Seablite

Another plant characteristic of the salt pans, and often found
behind mangroves, is Seablite, typically a low-growing herb

Suaeda australis (Seablite)

but sometimes a shrub up to 60 cm tall. Freshly produced foliage, and that in shaded positions, is a soft green, but the leaves tend to become pink or purplish and a sward of Seablite may appear rosy red from a distance.

The very succulent leaves are narrow and thick, up to 4 cm long but only 3 mm broad, and semicircular in section; they are alternate, rather crowded, and curved inwards towards their tips. Pleasantly salty to nibble fresh, they also make a useful cooked vegetable.

Flowers are produced in terminal sprays; they are small and green and are followed by small gritty-looking fruits.

Family Clusiaceae (Guttiferae)

Calophyllum inophyllum   Alexandrian Laurel

Calophyllum inophyllum is a distinctive tree, common from Cardwell northwards. The name *Calophyllum* is derived from the Greek *kalos* (beautiful), *phyllon* (leaf), a good choice of name in this case. The handsome leaves are opposite, more or less elliptical, with the rounded apex often notched; the texture is tough and rigid, the surface glossy, and running out from the midrib are the distinctive, closely placed parallel lateral veins. A yellowish latex flows from injuries.

Old trees may reach a height of nearly 20 m, and are often branched from near the base. In the Cape Tribulation area there are some particularly fine specimens, their bases lapped by high tides and the branches spreading widely over the beach, occasionally resting on one "elbow".

Calophyllum inophyllum
(Alexandrian Laurel)

The attractive, perfumed flowers 2–3 cm across have white petals and a mass of yellow stamens. These are followed by almost spherical grey-green fruits about the size of golf balls – and sounding like them if they land on the roof of a car or tent at night. The seeds are not edible, but a green oil can be extracted from them and, in the Indo-Pacific region, this has been used for lighting, soap-making, and a wide variety of medicinal purposes including the treatment of various skin disorders and rheumatism.

See also in chapter 6, "Flotsam".

Family Combretaceae

Terminalia arenicola   Beach Almond

Terminalias have been called Pagoda Trees because, in the sapling stage, the main lateral branches are approximately whorled on the main trunk and produce a tiered effect suggesting the eaves of a pagoda. Horizontal branches bend upwards to bear a dense rosette of leaves, and at the point of bending they branch to continue the lateral growth. Repeated growth of this type gives the characteristic layered effect in young trees. This form tends to be lost as the tree ages.

Terminalia arenicola is a sand-inhabiting species, as is implied by the second part of its botanical name, derived from the Latin *arena* (sand), and *incolere* (to inhabit). Its leaves broaden conspicuously towards the upper part, and in late winter or spring turn yellow or orange-red before falling and leaving the tree leafless or almost leafless before the new flush of leaves and small cream flowers. The fruits are of about the size and shape of an almond with shell, with a thin, fleshy purple covering which flying foxes appear to find attractive, but which is unpalatable to humans.

See also in chapter 6, "Flotsam".

Terminalia arenicola (Beach Almond)

Terminalia catappa Sea Almond, Indian Almond

Terminalia catappa, the Sea Almond or Indian Almond, is probably the best-known species of the genus, and although it is native to Australia the majority of specimens occurring along the Queensland coast have probably been planted. They are to be seen at many of the Reef island resorts and on the mainland foreshore. There are some fine examples along Queen's Beach at Bowen.

Leaves of *T. catappa* are very large, up to about 35 cm long and 20 cm wide; in winter the vivid "autumn"' colouring of deep crimson makes the tree stand out from a distance. The flowers are not showy, being small and white, produced in groups of slender sprays in spring while the previous year's fruit are still being shed.

The fruit, up to 10 cm long, is somewhat almond-shaped and at first has a thin purplish flesh surrounding the fibrous stone. It contains a slender kernel made up mainly of the closely coiled seed leaves. This is edible, with a flavour not unlike the almond, but is difficult to extract from its shell which does not crack apart as readily as does that of the almond. Seeds are most easily recovered by cutting the fruit in half with a tomahawk. Juice of the young leaves is used in parts of India to make an ointment for skin disease; the bark, which is astringent, has been used to treat dysentery.

See also in chapter 6, "Flotsam".

Terminalia catappa (Sea Almond, Indian Almond)

Family Convolvulaceae

Ipomoea macrantha   Moon Flower

Although often found near the beach, *Ipomoea macrantha* is not an early colonizer as is Goat's-foot Convolvulus. It appears, rather, amongst established vegetation over which it scrambles and twines, often hanging in festoons from near the tops of trees.

The large, white, funnel-shaped flowers open at night and collapse soon after dawn except on very dull days, when they persist a little longer. However, the sepals persist as fleshy, cream scale-like structures enclosing the fruit.

In the Gilbert Islands stems and leaves are crushed in water to prepare a shampoo which is believed to kill lice.

Ipomoea macrantha (Moon Flower)

Ipomoea pes-caprae subsp. *brasiliensis*   Goat's-foot
Convolvulus

Goat's-foot Convolvulus is often one of the earliest species to colonize newly deposited dunes, its rapidly elongating pro-strate stems quickly covering a wide area and effecting initial stabilization of the shifting sand. The bilobed leaf, suggesting

Ipomoea pes-caprae subsp. *brasiliensis* (Goat's-foot Convolvulus)

the outline of a cloven hoof, justifies the Latin epithet *pes-caprae* (goat's foot). Handsome, purple-pink, funnel-shaped flowers up to 6 cm across are borne singly in the leaf axils. Dry, almost papery fruits contain four very hairy seeds.

The fleshy tap root penetrates deep into the soil; in fact, it has been recorded up to nearly 3 m in length. After cooking, it is edible but is very fibrous and has some reputation of being purgative and diuretic if not used in moderation. In South-East Asia and the South Pacific the leaves have been made into poultices to treat boils, ulcers and snake bite, and the juice has been applied to fish stings.

Another purple-flowered *Ipomoea* found on a number of islands and shores is a garden escape, the Mile-a-Minute or Railway Creeper, *I. cairica*. This fast-growing creeper may be easily distinguished from Goat's-foot Convolvulus by its palmately lobed leaves of five to seven fingers.

Family Cyperaceae

Cyperus pedunculatus   Pineapple Sedge
(Remirea maritima)

Sedges are typically plants of moist places, but *Cyperus pedunculatus* is one which survives the frequently desiccated habitat of the maritime dunes. Its subterranean stems spread widely, giving rise to numerous short erect shoots which

Cyperus pedunculatus (Pineapple Sedge)

emerge from the sand like rows of miniature pineapple tops. The yellowish-green slender leaves are 5–10 cm long, rough edged, rigid, sharply pointed and best avoided by bare feet.

The inflorescence at the end of the flowering stalk is a dense group of brown spikelets surrounded by three to six leafy bracts which vary in length.

Family Dilleniaceae

Dillenia alata   Golden Guinea Tree

The Golden Guinea Tree is one of the most handsome of the trees on the tropical shore. Its stout trunk is freely branched to give a spreading canopy of rounded-elliptical leaves with eight to ten distinct, parallel lateral veins on each side of the midrib; the leaf stalk is prominently winged, with the wings on leaves at the branch apex folded together, sheathing the next leaf. Beautiful red papery bark is most distinctive in sheltered positions, where it can be peeled off in thin layers; on exposed trunks it tends to be harder, less red, and flaky rather than papery.

Dillenia alata (Golden Guinea Tree)

The flowers are brilliant. Five concave, fleshy calyx lobes surround the five bright yellow, delicately textured petals, which usually last less than a day. In the centre of the numerous stamens, the ovary is a ribbed red cone with seven or eight recurved tapering styles gradually fading to cream towards the apices. After the petals are shed the calyx closes on the developing fruit but spreads again at maturity; this allows the red fruit to split open, each of the seven or eight compartments revealing a single white seed.

Family Ebenaceae

Diospyros ferrea var. *reticulata*   Sea Ebony

Sea Ebony belongs to the group from which the very hard, heavy and dark ebony wood is obtained. However, this species does not reach sufficient size for it to be an important source of timber.

The plant suckers from the roots, so it tends to occur in small groves. Its clearly net-veined, leathery leaves, often with down-curved edges, have blunt apices frequently with an indentation.

The globose-elliptical fruit, about 1.5 cm broad, is seated on a three-lobed saucer formed by the persistent calyx. When fully ripe and red it is edible, but is very astringent if sampled in the yellow stage. This fruit is attractive to the Torres Strait Pigeon which nests during summer in enormous numbers on Low Isles off Port Douglas.

Diospyros ferrea var. *reticulata* (Sea Ebony)

Diospyros maritima   Native Persimmon

Although it occurs at many places along the coast, Green Island, where the species is particularly common, is probably

Diospyros maritima (Native Persimmon)

the place where most people will encounter this plant. The dark-green, glossy leaves are elongate egg-shaped in outline, up to 20 cm long, and are arranged alternately in two ranks so that final branches often have the appearance of large pinnate leaves. Its fruits, flattened-globose and about 2 cm across, resemble small fruits of Persimmon which also is a species of *Diospyros*. Initially green, they change through yellow to orange-red or brick-red. Soft flesh surrounding several seeds has a flavour at first resembling that of a Persimmon, but soon an additional unpleasant flavour becomes apparent and gives no encouragement to finishing a whole fruit.

Family Euphorbiaceae

Euphorbia   Spurge

The Euphorbias are easy plants to recognize, with their milky latex and distinctive floral structure. Numerous male flowers, each consisting of only a single stamen, and one female flower, also without sepals and petals, are packed together in a cup-like organ. The cup, in most cases, carries one to five flattened glands around its edge, so that the whole structure may look like a single flower rather than a group of flowers.

First to emerge from the cup is the three-lobed ovary with its six stigmas. This is carried up on a stalk which bends over to one side so that the ovary seems to be drooping out of the cup. Stamens emerge later, a few at a time. Eventually, the ovary stalk straightens again and the three lobes of the fruit break away, leaving behind the withered axis.

The milky latex of various species is sometimes applied to warts in the hope of causing their disappearance.

Euphorbia atoto

This is a prostrate species. Its pointed-ovate leaves are unequal-sided at the base and have a narrow purplish-pink

Euphorbia atoto

border. There are four yellow-green glands somewhat resembling petals around the edge of the cup.

Euphorbia cyathophora — Dwarf Poinsettia, Mexican Fire-plant

An immigrant from tropical America, this species is sometimes cultivated in Australia as an ornamental, but is much inferior to the closely related Poinsettia. On some of the islands it has become naturalized and it may form dense thickets up to 1.5 m high. Leaves are entire or with a couple of broad lobes on each side.

On each cup there is a single gland with something of the form of a pair of lips. The terminal cluster of flowering cups is surrounded by five to seven bracts, or modified leaves. The smaller of these bracts are wholly red, but the larger have only a red basal patch.

Euphorbia cyathophora (Dwarf Poinsettia, Mexican Fire-plant)

Euphorbia tannensis

Often accompanying *Euphorbia atoto* close to the beach, this species is readily distinguished by its erect form, 30–50 cm high, and its distinct main stem. Slender opposite leaves, four

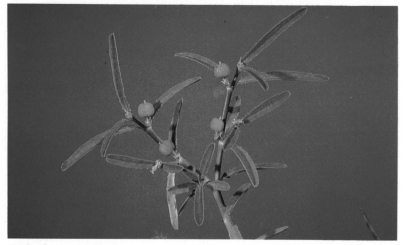

Euphorbia tannensis

or five times as long as broad, may carry a few teeth along their length, but more often there are a few prominent teeth at the base and three at the apex. The flowering cups are similar to those of *E. atoto*.

Macaranga tanarius   Tumkullum

This small tree, which occurs in a wide range of areas, from rainforest margins to seashores, is perhaps not exciting in appearance, but is readily recognized. The leaves are mostly ovate with a drawn-out apex, and may be up to 30 cm in length; some are three-lobed. A distinctive feature is the long pinkish leaf stalk inserted within the margin of the blade, the main veins radiating from this point; on the pale under-surface of the leaf the veins show a regular rectangular pattern.

Separate male and female flowers are individually small, but are borne in clusters surrounded by fringed bracts. The soft-spined fruit is pea-sized and contains three seeds.

Although regarded as commercially useless in Australia, the plant has been exploited in various ways in South-East Asia. A gum obtained by tapping the trunk provides a glue used in making musical instruments such as guitars; the wood, which is white and light, has been cut to make diving

Macaranga tanarius (Tumkullum)

goggles in the Philippines. The bark is a source of tannin which can be extracted for toughening fishing nets or for preparing medicine to treat dysentery.

When injured, the tissues exude a latex which has been used in north Queensland as a styptic, a substance which checks bleeding.

Family Fabaceae

Abrus precatorius   Jequirity, Rosary Pea,
                                              Crab's Eye

This slender perennial climber occurs naturally throughout the tropics; it is an attractive plant, with fresh, green pinnate leaves of up to fifteen pairs of leaflets each 10–12 mm long. Tight clusters of rather small, pink pea-flowers are followed by handsome fruits which are the most striking feature of the plant. Grey-brown pods twist as they open to reveal a short row of scarlet seeds each with a large black spot at the lower end; these are persistent on the plant, and the radiating pods with brilliant seeds make an eye-catching display.

The seeds are extremely poisonous, half a seed having been fatal to an adult who chewed it; if introduced into the bloodstream even a minute amount is lethal. However, the seed-coat is very hard, and a whole seed swallowed would probably pass through the body unbroken. In many countries the seeds have been used as beads for necklaces and rosaries; the Aborigines used them ornamentally on some weapons. They were also used as standard weights by early Indian goldsmiths.

Although the seeds are poisonous, the leaves are not; in fact, they have been used as a tonic and are pleasant to chew fresh.

Abrus precatorius (Jequirity, Rosary Pea, Crab's Eye)

Canavalia rosea   Fire Bean, Sea Bean

Among the strand plants are several long-stemmed prostrate species which spread over a considerable area, helping to stabilize the sand surface. One of the most common of these is the Fire Bean, its long stems, usually prostrate but sometimes twining, bearing alternate trifoliate leaves with broadly elliptical leaflets.

The mauve pea-flowers are carried in groups of two to twenty on a long flowering stalk; they are unusual in that they appear upside-down, with the standard, the largest petal, lowermost. Green pods, about 10 cm long, contain about eight seeds embedded in a pithy membrane, and these are edible after cooking although poisonous when raw. The whole pod is edible if young enough, again, only after cooking. Mature seeds shed from the pods are extremely hard.

Canavalia rosea (Fire Bean, Sea Bean)

Dalbergia candenatensis

This is a woody climber found along some quiet shorelines, particularly at the junction of mangroves and terrestrial forests. Its pinnate leaves have usually four to six alternately arranged leaflets, either elliptical or broader towards the

Dalbergia candenatensis

apex. The small pea-flowers are not conspicuous. A most distinctive feature of the plant is the occurrence of contorted tendril-like structures formed by some of the tough brown stems.

Dendrolobium umbellatum

In northern Queensland, *Dendrolobium umbellatum* is a common shrub of the strand, sometimes sprawling at high-

Dendrolobium umbellatum

water mark. The trifoliate leaves, with leaflets 6–10 cm long, are greyish on the underside because of the presence of closely appressed hairs which also give the young shoots a silky appearance. Groups of six to twelve small, white, pea-flowers arise near the apex of a short stalk in the leaf axil. The distinctive flattened pods, about 1 cm broad, are usually curved and much-constricted on the convex side between each of the two to five seeds; fragmentation into one-seeded segments occurs readily.

Young leaves are said to be used as a vegetable in parts of South-East Asia; however they are somewhat astringent.

Derris trifoliata

Although its name suggests otherwise, leaves of this species are mostly pinnate with five elliptical leaflets 6–10 cm long, slightly heart-shaped at the base. The plant is a twiner, but in the absence of support often scrambles over the ground. It produces sprays of pea-flowers, white with a pale blush of pinkish lavender and about 1 cm long. Pods are flattened and kidney-shaped. The well-known insecticide, derris dust, is derived from the roots of some species of *Derris*; *D. trifoliata* has been used as an insecticide in South-East Asia but in Australia its only use seems to have been by the Aborigines, as a fish poison.

Derris trifoliata

Erythrina variegata   Coral Tree

When in flower, the Coral Tree is perhaps the most brilliant tree along the tropical shore. Coming into bloom in early summer when the tree is leafless, it produces conical trusses of scarlet pea-flowers which make an eye-catching display. The flowers tend to be grouped in whorls of six to nine. Each flower has a single large petal, the standard, about 7 cm long, and four smaller petals; the ten stamens are partly fused in a tube around the protruding style.

Erythrina variegata (Coral Tree)

Even when not flowering, the tree is easily recognized, having pale corky bark studded with long rows of lenticels giving it a striated appearance; sometimes there are a few persistent prickles on the main trunk, and there are always plenty on the branches. The long-stalked leaves have three large leaflets about 15 cm broad and a little less in length, varying from diamond-shaped to rounded. Pods contain attractive red seeds.

This species is one of the Coral Trees in cultivation as an ornamental. It is poisonous but has been used medicinally in Asia in a variety of ways.

Mucuna gigantea   Velvet Bean

Like many other climbing plants, the Velvet Bean is not readily noticed unless in flower or fruit; the trifoliate leaves tend to be hidden high in the trees over which the vine grows. However, the flowers are unusual and handsome; light green in colour, the fist-sized clusters of pea-flowers, 4 cm long, hang like chandeliers on stems up to a metre long. Apart from the green petals, the flowers are memorable for the very sharp, fine, light-brown hairs coating the pouched calyx; these lie flat against the surface and are very easily but uncomfortably detached.

The flower cluster is followed by a group of almost black, flattened pods up to 14 cm long, also hanging on the long stem; each of the pod's narrow edges is marked by two wing-like ridges. Although the pod is visually fairly distinctive it is its physical impact which makes the more lasting impression; the pod is sparsely covered with rusty hairs similar to those on the calyx and these are easily picked up by enquiring fingers to which they impart considerable discomfort. This displeasing feature of the plant has been put to criminal use in Malaysia where the hairs have been used as a poison.

Mucuna gigantea (Velvet Bean)

Each pod contains from two to five flattened black seeds with a matt surface almost resembling charcoal.

See also in chapter 6, "Flotsam".

Pongamia pinnata   Indian Beech

Pongamia pinnata is a small tree with graceful arching branches which has been used to some extent in ornamental planting in Queensland.

The pinnate leaves have usually three pairs of leaflets and a terminal leaflet. Indian Beech is one of the relatively few deciduous trees in Queensland; the bare period, however, is fairly short. The pea-flowers are white and pale pink. Pods are about 5 cm long, roughly twice as long as broad, and most contain only one seed.

All parts of the plant are reported to be toxic and strongly emetic if taken internally. However, a reddish oil extracted from the seeds has been used in the Indo-Pacific region for treating skin diseases and rheumatism; friends of ours from India report using it with great success on their buffalo when she had a severe skin infection. Australian Aborigines used the pounded roots as an effective fish poison which did not affect the edible quality of the catch.

Pongamia pinnata (Indian Beech)

Sophora tomentosa   Silver Bush

Soft silvery-grey pinnate leaves with up to fifteen leaflets make Silver Bush an easily recognized shrub of the strand. Bright-yellow pea-flowers are followed by long pods, also grey at first; these are so strongly constricted between the ten or so seeds that the pods look almost like strings of beads.

Sophora tomentosa (Silver Bush)

The globular shiny seeds and yellow bark of the roots have been used medicinally in the Malaysian-Pacific region for the treatment of illness resulting from eating poisonous fish, while the pounded leaves have been applied to wounds caused by venomous fish. Other medicinal uses have been in the treatment of diarrhoea, cholera and hepatitis. However, the alkaloid the plant contains is strongly emetic and purgative, and is poisonous in large quantities, so would not be the first choice as a medicine.

Vigna marina

Vigna marina is a creeping strand bean with trifoliate leaves, very similar in appearance to the Fire Bean, *Canavalia rosea*,

Vigna marina

which is found in similar situations. In flower, it can be readily be distinguished from *C. rosea* by its yellow rather than purplish pea-flowers.

Family Goodeniaceae

Scaevola sericea
(S. taccada)

Cardwell Cabbage,
Native Cabbage,
Sea Lettuce Tree

Along the strand, *Scaevola sericea* occurs sometimes as scattered shrubs, sometimes as an almost impenetrable hedge separating the grasses and herbs at the top of the beach from the forest behind. Its bright green, shiny leaves are broadest in the upper part and taper gradually to a very short leaf stalk which has a group of silky hairs in its axil; on the rounded upper part of the leaf are three to thirteen small, purplish marginal glands. In the bud, and commonly in the adult, the leaf margins curve downwards. When the leaf falls it leaves a prominent crescent-shaped scar on the green or purplish stem. Rapidly growing branches have their leaves widely separated but, as growth slows, the leaves become grouped in a terminal cluster; as such leaves fall, the scars they leave behind are overlapping and produce a snakeskin-like pattern on the branch.

The common names suggest edibility, and the leaves reportedly have been cooked and eaten in Hawaii. However, we find them bitter and unacceptable.

The short flowering cluster has the type of branching, termed cymose, in which the axis terminates in a flower and growth is continued by one or a pair of branches arising at the base of its stalk. For this reason flowers often occur in pairs. Flowers are white or often flushed with purple. Each of the five petals has a "reinforcing" strip down the back with a membranous wing on each side of it. Down one side, the flower is deeply split, almost as though part of it had been torn away, and the petals are spread out like a fan. Opposite the split the bowed style with its brush-like tip is prominent.

There is a vague resemblance in the flower to an outstretched hand, and it is this resemblance, together with the brownish scorched appearance of spent flowers, which prompted the naming of the plant as *Scaevola*. According to legend, in 507 BC the Roman Gaius Mucius attempted to kill Lars Porsena, who was besieging Rome. On being captured and threatened with death, Gaius Mucius, to show he was

Scaevola sericea (Cardwell Cabbage, Native Cabbage, Sea Lettuce Tree)

not afraid, thrust his right hand into the altar fire and kept it there. Much impressed, Lars Porsena freed the captive who, from that time on, was known as Scaevola in reference to his left-handedness.

Five narrow erect sepals crown the white or cream rounded fruit, which is about 1 cm across and sometimes faintly ribbed. The juice of the fleshy layer surrounding the smooth seed is reputedly soothing to inflamed eyes. Although the fruit are eaten by Grey-breasted Silvereyes they are bitter and unpalatable to human taste.

In the Malaysian region, the pith of the stem has been used for the making of rice paper and small ornaments. In the Queensland plants the pith, although well developed, is hardly large enough for this purpose. In dried stems it con-tracts to form a row of small pithy discs.

Family Hernandiaceae

Hernandia peltata   Sea Hearse

Although trees of *Hernandia peltata* are not particularly common along the shore they are very distinctive. The leaf blade, 15–30 cm long, is egg-shaped but tapering to a point, and has its stalk inserted some distance from the margin. In the sprays of small flowers each female flower is flanked by two males. The fruit is a hard, black rounded structure up to 2.5 cm across, marked with eight to ten longitudinal ridges.

Hernandia peltata (Sea Hearse)

Surrounding it is the particularly distinctive feature of the plant, a loose, smooth cream envelope with a circular opening at the top through which the black fruit can be seen. The common name is one used in Malaysia for a very closely related species, the fruit's structure apparently suggesting a carved coffin surrounded by a pale shroud.

The seeds are very oily, and at one time were used to a limited extent in Indonesia as a candle substitute in much the same way as were those of the Candle-nut.

Family Hippocrateaceae

Salacia chinensis   Lolly Berry

The original Salacia was said to be the wife of Neptune, and this plant namesake keeps that association with the sea. A common woody climber along shores of the far north, it is conspicuous when in fruit, but liable to be overlooked at other times. However, it has an interesting feature: as well as the expected turns of a twining stem, it throws lateral branches which coil around a support close to the parent stem and then grow straight, so a branch may do a 180⁰ turn and grow in the opposite direction from the way it emerged. The leaves are opposite, entire, elliptical and variable in size.

Salacia chinensis (Lolly Berry)

Flowers are small, with five rather narrow yellow petals which fold back as the flower ages. Between the petals and the stamens is a raised thickened disc; this is a nectar gland. The fruits are globose or pear-shaped, 2–3 cm in diameter, and bright orange-red; they are edible and pleasant, although the proportion of pulp is not high.

Roots of Lolly Berry have been used in Indian traditional medicine to treat diabetes.

Family Lauraceae

Cassytha filiformis Dodder Laurel,
Devil's Twine, Devil's Guts

The slender leafless stems of this parasite grow without contact with the soil, twining and climbing over other plants and driving small parasitic roots into the host. Sometimes a group of stems will be twined round each other to form a rough rope; sometimes a layer of stems, as hopelessly tangled as a discarded fishing line, will form a smothering shroud which almost obscures the host beneath. It is found generally in well-illuminated positions, often overgrowing grasses and shrubs close to the beach.

In the plant world, this species is probably the nearest thing to a cannibal. When branches of *Cassytha* twine together or cross one another, each may penetrate the other with its parasitic roots.

Plants exposed to full sunlight commonly develop a yellow or orange colour but shaded plants are green, indicating the presence of chlorophyll and the ability to photosynthesize. However, the parasite is completely dependent on the host for water and mineral nutrients.

Small cream flowers are followed by round white fruits,

Cassytha filiformis (Dodder Laurel, Devil's Twine, Devil's Guts)

nearly a centimetre across, which take on a translucent appearance when ripe. The fleshy layer is edible but only mildly enjoyable.

In Fiji, this plant has provided a treatment for indigestion, while in India the dried material mixed with oil has been applied as a hair tonic. There is little strength in the stems and they can be used for twine only for minor and temporary purposes such as the stringing of flowers into garlands, as is done in the Gilbert Islands.

Family Lecythidaceae

Barringtonia asiatica   Box Fruit

A handsome tree of the tropical western Pacific, *Barringtonia asiatica* has large glossy leaves, exceptionally up to 60 cm long, broadest in their upper part and tapering to an almost stalkless base. The lower part of the midrib is usually pink, and on the undersurface the main veins are prominently raised. Its large striking flowers up to 15 cm across are strictly nocturnal; buds start to swell about midday, the enclosing calyx is split into two or three parts, and the flowers open at dusk revealing a mass of beautiful stamens, white below, pink above. By dawn next day the rings of stamens are lying over the ground, still beautiful but rapidly deteriorating. There is a somewhat musty scent to the flowers, which are reported to be pollinated by moths hovering in front of the flowers as they insert their long proboscis.

The distinctive fibrous fruits, something like small four-angled coconuts, are often washed up on beaches.

This species has played a part in fishing activities of some Pacific native peoples, the buoyant fruits being used as fishing net floats, and the pounded seed, fruit or bark being thrown into pools to stupefy fish. Saponin is the active principle.

See also in chapter 6, "Flotsam".

Barringtonia asiatica (Box Fruit)

Planchonia careya   Cocky Apple

Although by no means restricted to coastal districts, Cocky Apple is often seen close to the beach. A small tree with crooked branching, it bears leaves about 7 cm wide, broadest in their upper part, which turn a bright orange-red before falling. The flowers are nocturnal and have much in common with those of *Barringtonia asiatica* although they are considerably smaller. A beautiful brush of stamens, pink below and white above, is the conspicuous part of the flower but mostly this falls from the tree about dawn.

When ripe, the greenish, egg-shaped fruit contains a fleshy material resembling cooked egg yolk among fibrous strands, and this is pleasant enough to eat in small quantities. Aborigines have used the pounded bark for poisoning fish.

Planchonia careya
(Cocky Apple)

Family Liliaceae

Crinum pedunculatum   Crinum Lily

Of the several species of *Crinum* in Australia, *C. pedunculatum* is the largest and the only one to develop a short "trunk", up to 60 cm tall, formed mainly by the closely wrapped leaf bases. Large sword-like leaves, often a metre long, spread roughly in a rosette at the apex of the "trunk".

Crinum pedunculatum (Crinum Lily)

Crinum pedunculatum (Crinum Lily)

The flowering stalk bears an umbel of twenty or more handsome, white lily-like flowers, each with a slender tube up to 10 cm long. The anthers swing freely on their purple filaments at the slightest disturbance, probably aiding the dispersal of the pollen.

When the shining green fruit splits, it releases about nine rounded-angular grey-green seeds, variable in size, · and unusual in having a corky covering but no seed-coat. Dispersal is mainly by water currents.

As well as growing close to beaches, this species is sometimes found in the uppermost intertidal region along brackish creeks, frequently associated with mangroves. The plant is readily cultivated and is often found around habitations.

Crushed leaves of Crinum Lily have been used in north Queensland to rub on stings of the notorious Box Jellyfish.

See also in chapter 6, "Flotsam".

Family Lythraceae

Pemphis acidula

At first sight this shrub might be mistaken for one of the Tea-trees (*Leptospermum* spp.) so common in Australia, but the flowers immediately distinguish the two, those of *Pemphis* having six rather than five petals. A common characteristic of members of the family to which *Pemphis* belongs is the crumpling of the petals in the bud so that the expanded petals appear wrinkled and ruffled; this character is even more prominent in the well-known garden tree, Pride of India (*Lagerstroemia indica*), which belongs to the same family.

The small, opposite, elliptical leaves, 1-2 cm long, are silky- haired and crowded on the twigs.

A typical position for *P. acidula* is in crevices between boulders where the plants may be reached by waves during very rough weather. Here they may take on a gnarled or distorted form, with the robust contorted roots firmly wedged in the rock crannies.

The leaves are acid to the taste and are reported to be edible. The wood is so hard that it has been used in India to make objects such as pestles and anchors.

Pemphis acidula

Family Malvaceae

Abutilon albescens   Lantern Bush

This small shrub, often about a metre in height, is readily recognized by its broad, deeply heart-shaped leaves, with the lobes at the top of the heart often overlapping. The pale green leaves have a peculiar and distinctive surface texture, almost like that of fine suede, due to the presence of closely placed, soft, star-shaped hairs.

The beautiful cupped flowers, bright orange-yellow in colour, are about 4 cm across, and have a structure akin to that of *Hibiscus* or Hollyhock. Male parts are united into a short central tube which divides into five lobes, each with a tuft of stamens at the tip; numerous free styles pass up through this staminal tube. The life of these flowers is a short one; usually they open about noon, and by dusk the petals have closed again. Next day they are spent and starting to wrinkle.

The five-lobed green calyx persists, and surrounds the fruit which, at maturity, is a densely hairy, ribbed structure vaguely resembling a broad cogged wheel. When dry, each of the approximately two dozen "cogs" splits along its narrow upper side to release three black kidney-shaped seeds.

Abutilon albescens (Lantern Bush)

A mucilaginous substance found in *Abutilon albescens*, as well as in many other members of the family, has been used in South-East Asia to prepare a soothing tonic. The tough fibrous bark can be retted to produce a fibre suitable for ropes, but it has not been used commercially.

Hibiscus tiliaceus   Cotton Tree

Hibiscus tiliaceus is a small spreading tree, sometimes with low interlaced branches forming a dense barrier close to the beach. Numerous microscopic hairs give the undersurface of the heart-shaped leaves a pale grey appearance.

The flowers are similar in structure to, but smaller than, those of the widely cultivated *H. rosa-sinensis* familiar to gardeners in warm climates. From the purple-red eye at the centre of the yellow flower arises a central tube bearing numerous short-stalked anthers; from the apex of this tube emerge the five dark purple stigmas. The flowers are spent on the afternoon of the day on which they open, and next morning are found on the ground below, fully open and with the colour much changed to dull orange-pink.

The hairy fruit is mainly enclosed within the persistent calyx lobes.

As in the case of most species of *Hibiscus*, the buds and

Hibiscus tiliaceus (Cotton Tree)

young shoots are edible after boiling or steaming. The bark yields a fibre of good quality which has been extensively used by the Aborigines for fishing lines and nets. Many other Pacific people have used the fibre for similar purposes; in Samoa it has been used for straining kava and for making foot coverings for walking on coral reefs. Another Samoan use of the plant was in making fire by friction, the *Hibiscus* wood being the softer of the two timbers used in the process. In Tonga, chewed leaves and a solution prepared from pounded bark and water are used to treat skin diseases; possibly the mucilaginous material commonly occurring in members of this family has a soothing effect.

Although not an important timber, Cotton Tree wood is durable in sea water and has been used in Pacific islands and in South-East Asia for light boats and some building purposes.

Thespesia populnea   Portia Tree, Indian Tulip Tree

Often accompanying *Hibiscus tiliaceus* on tropical strands is a related and closely similar plant, *Thespesia populnea*. However, there are several characters on which the two can readily be distinguished. The heart-shaped leaves of *Thespesia* lack white hairs on the undersurface. Although the

Thespesia populnea (Portia Tree, Indian Tulip Tree)

yellow flowers of the two are similar in many respects, *Thespesia* has a yellow undivided stigma rather than five purple stigmas protruding from the staminal column. Spent flowers of *Thespesia* usually remain on the plant longer than those of *H. tiliaceus*. In *Thespesia* the rounded-flattened fruit is not enclosed by the calyx, which in this genus forms a disc-like structure at its base.

The Portia Tree is an attractive ornamental tree. It is not of economic importance in Australia, but has a wide variety of local uses in southern Asia and the Pacific islands; the timber is used for tool handles and building purposes, as a source of tannin and as fuel; bark, leaves, flowers and fruits are used medicinally for skin diseases and intestinal complaints; the leaves provide food for people and domestic animals; flowers and fruits yield a yellow dye; and the bark provides a strong fibre.

Urena lobata   Pink Burr

Pink Burr is one of those herbs, dismissed as weeds, which pass unnoticed unless they are in flower. The leaves are three- to five-lobed, broader than long, and have five large and two small veins radiating from the base of the leaf. The young stems and both surfaces of the leaves are covered with star-shaped hairs.

Urena lobata (Pink Burr)

Flowers are of the *Hibiscus* type, 3–4 cm across, of a delicate pink with a darker eye. In the centre is a pink staminal tube, dividing at the apex to produce numerous anthers on short filaments; at maturity these produce masses of extremely large, pale grey pollen grains. Protruding from the tube are ten red stigmas, each with a halo of pale hairs. The fruit is a five-lobed burr a little more than 1 cm in diameter; this is covered with hooked bristles like minute anchors which aid in distribution.

Like other members of the family, *Urena lobata* is rich in mucilage; it has been used in South-East Asia to prepare a soothing medicine taken for dysentery. The bark fibre is strong and can be used like jute for rope and sacking.

Family Meliaceae

Aglaia elaeagnoidea

This small tree with alternate pinnate leaves with three or five leaflets is easily recognized by the dense layer of silvery-brown scales on both sides of young leaves. Older leaves lose most of the scales from their upper surface. Sprays of small flowers are followed by rounded fruits, up to 1.5 cm across, densely covered with shiny scales.

Aglaia elaeagnoidea

Family Mimosaceae

Entada phaseoloides   Matchbox Bean

The most striking feature of this woody climber is its fruit, a huge bean up to about 120 cm in length; these pods often hang high in a supporting tree on the tropical shoreline. At maturity the pod may break into one-seeded segments; these may be shed leaving the stout "strings" of the bean hanging as an empty frame from the vine. The glossy, flat brown seeds, not unlike chocolate-coated biscuits in size and appearance, are the "matchboxes" of the common name; in colonial times they were used to make highly ornamental containers for wax matches.

Plants climb by tendrils which are found in pairs at the end of many of the compound leaves. Individual leaflets may be 8 cm or more in length, and the lower half of each is slightly larger than the upper so that the leaflet is curved forwards.

Entada phaseoloides
(Matchbox Bean)

Entada phaseoloides (Matchbox Bean)

Flowers are produced in feathery spikes 20 cm or more in length, something like an enormous *Acacia* spike; they are white at first, becoming yellow as they age, and have a strong, sweet, but rather unpleasant, scent. Individuals of the very numerous flowers have short, dark red sepals and petals but the conspicuous part of the flower is its ten stamens, each about 7 mm long.

Although the seeds are toxic, they have been used by the Aborigines as food after prolonged treatment. The plant is rich in saponins which produce a lather, and stems have been widely used in South-East Asia for shampoo.

See also in chapter 6, "Flotsam".

Mimosa pudica   Sensitive Plant

Although an American native, the Sensitive Plant has become widespread throughout the tropics, and is frequently found beside walking tracks on the islands, as well as on the mainland.

Sprawling reddish stems bear scattered, hard, recurved prickles, also occurring at the leaf bases. The leaf axis has four branches arising in close proximity, each bearing numerous small leaflets about 1 cm long. These leaves are probably the most interesting feature of the plant: they

Mimosa pudica (Sensitive Plant)

respond to a touch or even to shaking by the wind by rapidly closing, each leaflet overlapping the next one forwards. If the stimulus is slight a few leaflets only may move, but with a stronger blow the whole leaf folds, bending rapidly downwards. The movement, the speed of which is unusual in plants, is due to water-pressure changes in the pulvinus, the swollen base of the leaf. Recovery is slow but discernible, taking less than fifteen minutes. The leaves also close at night; this "sleep" behaviour has given rise, in parts of South-East Asia, to the belief that the plant can induce sleep in humans; pieces of the plant are placed under the sleeping mat of a fretful child in the hope that both child and parents will get a good night's rest.

Flowers of the Sensitive Plant are very attractive; the fluffy lilac-pink balls, about 2 cm in diameter, are similar in structure to those of some species of *Acacia* (wattle). Numerous lilac-coloured stamens screen the minute red petals at the centre. Each flower may develop a pod, so the flower-head is followed by a cluster of perhaps two dozen dry pods about 1.5 cm long, each with bristly hairs forming a fringe around its margin. The pod is strongly constricted between the three or four seeds and, at maturity when the fruit has changed from green through red to brown, single-seeded segments are shed, leaving behind the bristly framework of the pod.

Although it is *Mimosa pudica* which is usually seen, there is a native Sensitive Plant, *Neptunia gracilis*. This is a low-growing plant more characteristic of inland areas, but is sometimes found along the coast. It has twice-pinnate leaves and small rounded heads of pale yellow flowers, less showy than those of the introduced species. The leaves are sensitive in much the same way as those of *M. pudica*.

Family Moraceae

Ficus drupacea   Red Fig

Several of the native species of *Ficus*, which are usually rain-forest inhabitants, occur along the shores of the tropical mainland and the northern islands. For example, it is not uncommon to see *F. benjamina*, the Weeping Fig, in such areas. Among the figs along the shore, *F. drupacea* stands out because of its unusually shaped fruit; it is conspicuous on Green Island as well as along the mainland coast.

Red Figs are large trees whose elongate-elliptical leaves are about 20 cm long, pale-veined and usually with a distinctly pointed apex. The stalkless fruits are ellipsoid or almost barrel-shaped, 2–2.5 cm long and produced in pairs; they change from yellowish green to orange-red when ripe.

Ficus drupacea (Red Fig)

Ficus obliqua var. *petiolaris*   Strangling Fig

Strangling Figs are typically rainforest plants and, as such, can be expected on some of the northern mainland islands, but one of them, *Ficus obliqua* var. *petiolaris*, is found also on some coral cays. Seeds dispersed by birds lodge in humus-

Ficus obliqua var. *petiolaris* (Strangling Fig) — the root mass enclosing a supporting trunk

containing crevices in branches, where they germinate, producing remarkably vigorous root growth from a small supply of nutrients. Although not parasitic, fig roots grow downwards along the supporting trunk, finally reaching the ground when growth is greatly accelerated. Further roots descend and branch, and wherever roots cross one another they fuse forming an irregular, latticed cylinder encasing the trunk like a corset. Eventually the support dies, probably mainly because of its inability to lay down new tissues within the constricting cage of roots. The supporting trunk then rots away, leaving the fig "trunk" consisting of a mass of fused roots.

As in the case of all figs, the bud at the apex of each branch is sheathed by two conspicuous tapering stipules forming a narrow cone; this can be eaten after cooking. Fruits are of the typical fig type, but little more than a centimetre in diameter. When ripe they are yellow or reddish, soft and edible.

Ficus opposita   Sandpaper Fig

One of the numerous native figs of Australia, *Ficus opposita* is a small, semideciduous tree with mostly opposite leaves. It sometimes suffers badly from depredations of the Fig Beetle,

Ficus opposita (Sandpaper Fig)

while the trunk is often attacked by borers, so it is not unusual to find the tree looking anything but the picture of health.

Adult leaves are ovate or elliptical, sometimes heart-shaped at the base, and may bear tar-like spots of the fungus *Phyllachora rhytismoides.* Some leaves on juvenile plants may be relatively long and slender with a couple of basal lobes, and bear only slight resemblance to the adult condition. Although some leaves are almost smooth, most have a rough sandpapery surface due to the presence of short rigid hairs. In some species of Sandpaper Fig the leaves are so harsh the Aborigines were able to use them for the final smoothing of wooden weapons.

The fruits are borne singly or in pairs in the leaf axils and resemble domestic figs except for their smaller size, 2–3 cm diameter. As they develop they take on a reddish-brown colour, and finally the fruits become purple-black and so softly succulent that the skin slides off between the fingers as it is picked. In this condition it is well worth eating, but it is only occasionally that one comes across such fruit; Grey-breasted Silvereyes, which are common birds on many of the islands, are much quicker than people at finding and consuming them.

Family Myoporaceae

Mypoporum acuminatum   Boobiella

Myporum acuminatum is a very variable species; it sometimes reaches the stature of a small tree, but on windswept headlands is a low, often windsheared or prostrate shrub. Its shiny leaves taper to both base and apex. The white flowers, occurring in small axillary groups, are tubular with five lobes, the throat bearing numerous hairs. Its fleshy rounded fruits, only a few millimetres across, are purplish when ripe.

Myoporum acuminatum (Boobiella)

Family Myrtaceae

Eugenia reinwardtiana   Coast Lilly-pilly
(*E. carissoides*)

Typically, *Eugenia reinwardtiana* is found as low spreading
shrubs among rocks, often not far from the waterline. The
glossy opposite leaves are broadly elliptical, about 3 x 2 cm,
sometimes with a yellowish tinge, especially on the undersurface. Four-petalled white flowers with numerous stamens
are single or in pairs in the leaf axils, and are sometimes carried on a short stalk. Round red berries, about 1-2 cm in
diameter, have one seed or sometimes two; the fruit are
pleasantly acid to eat.

Eugenia reinwardtiana (Coast Lilly-pilly)

Most of the Australian lilly-pillies, once treated as members
of the genus *Eugenia*, have now been transferred to *Acmena*
and *Syzygium*, so that *E. reinwardtiana* remains as the sole
Australian representative of *Eugenia*. The arrangement of its
flowers singly or in pairs in the leaf axils readily distinguishes
the Coast Lilly-pilly from other lilly-pillies, whose flowers are
borne in branched sprays.

Melaleuca leucadendra   Weeping Tea-tree

In tropical eastern Queensland *Melaleuca leucadendra* is a very common tree fringing freshwater streams and gullies, and is commonly seen close to the shore where streams enter the sea. The tree is a particularly beautiful one, especially when seen reflected in the calm surface of a stream with its pale, almost white, paperbark trunks supporting the graceful pendulous branchlets and leaves. Oil glands are clearly seen by transmitted light in the elongate, often slightly curved leaves. The white to cream flowers are arranged in a bottle-brush and have a delightful caramel scent.

Melaleuca leucadendra
(Weeping Tea-tree)

Melaleuca viridiflora   Broad-leaved Tea-tree

This species is seen near the shore mainly on swampy ground, often associated with sedges and sedge-like plants close to mangroves. Another paper-barked species, it differs

Melaleuca viridiflora (Broad-leaved Tea-tree)

from *Melaleuca leucadendra* in its rather crooked, non-pendulous branches and shorter, more rigid leaves. The bottle-brush flowering spike varies in colour from white through creamy green and pink to red.

Family Nyctaginaceae

Boerhavia tetrandra
(B. albiflora)

From the top of a white, carroty tap root the prostrate stems of this herb diverge, bearing shiny, almost hairless leaves with a silvery lower surface.

The long flowering stalk usually divides two or three times, each final branch ending in a cluster of small, almost stalkless white flowers. Fruits are barrel-shaped, only about 3mm long, with five longitudinal ribs. Between these ribs are numerous minute, short-stalked glands whose sticky exudate causes the ripe fruit to adhere to any sock or hairy leg which brushes against it.

Boerhavia tetrandra

Commicarpus insularum   Gum Fruit

This slender, weakly scrambling herb reaches to about a metre in height if some support is available to it. The triangular to heart-shaped leaves are borne in well-spaced opposite pairs, and mostly have a dull appearance due to the presence of numerous hairs.

Alternately along the crooked stem in one axil of each pair

Commicarpus insularum (Gum Fruit)

of leaves a slender flowering stalk arises and bears at its apex a cluster of small flowers, up to eight in number. In some cases, the axis of the flowering stalk continues growth through the first cluster and produces a second one further up. These flowers are short-stalked, white or pale pink and trumpet-shaped. When they first open, the style and three stamens are irregularly bent and coiled but gradually straighten and protrude beyond the petals.

The elongate fruit, 8–10 mm long, gradually broadening upwards, is marked by ten longitudinal ridges. Near the apex of each ridge is a small knob. These are alternately at slightly different heights so that the double ring of knobs caps the fruit almost like a coronet. At maturity, the glandular head of each knob produces a sticky exudate which aids in the dispersal of the fruits by animals. It is to these knobs that the genus owes its Greek-derived name: *commi* (gum), *carpos* (fruit).

Pisonia grandis   Pisonia

When Matthew Flinders in the *Investigator* landed on Bountiful Island in the Gulf of Carpentaria in December 1802, he was delighted by the addition to the ship's larder of forty-six turtles. Robert Brown, the expedition's botanist,

Pisonia grandis (Pisonia)

Pisonia grandis (Pisonia) –
fruits

made an equally interesting discovery, though no doubt one less appreciated at the time; he made the first collection of *Pisonia grandis*.

This tree has an interesting distribution. It is widespread in the Indo-Pacific region from the Seychelles in the west to Pitcairn Island in the east, its northern and southern limits being marked almost exactly by the Tropics of Cancer and Capricorn. Except where it has been cultivated for food or as an ornamental, as it has in parts of the Malaysian region, it is usually restricted to small, often uninhabited islands with large bird populations. It is on such sites, coral cays with their vast sea-bird populations, that Pisonia is found along the Queensland coast.

Pisonia may occur in almost pure stands, with the largest trees reaching a height of 20 m. The distinctive, smooth, pale-barked trunks typically have a waist at a height of about 1 m, and from the broadened base below it some trees produce several slender shoots. Branches are exceptionally brittle and spongy and often unequal to the task of supporting the dense canopy; even on calm days one may occasionally hear the crash of a falling branch followed by the distressed cries of startled birds.

The broad leaves are large and soft, sometimes up to 50 cm long, with sharply contrasting cream-coloured midrib and main lateral veins; at its base, the leaf blade is often asymmetrical. Leaves exposed to full sunlight have a yellowish-green colour, very distinctive when the foliage is viewed from a distance and contrasted with that of other trees. The whole tree often has a somewhat battered appearance, due partly to the combined effect of strong winds and brittle stems, and partly to leaf loss in dry weather − during prolonged spells without rain the trees are semideciduous.

The clustered, sweetly scented, small greenish flowers are either male or female and, although usually borne on different trees, may sometimes be found on the same branch.

Female flowers are followed by club-shaped brown fruits, about 1 cm long, each with five longitudinal rows of warts. Along these rows appears a resinous, sticky exudate which is unaffected by water, and it is this exudate which leads each year to the death of many hundreds of sea birds as the ripening of the fruits and the nesting of the birds coincide.

Worst affected is usually the Black Noddy, better known as

the White-capped Noddy (*Anous minutus*), which not only nests on the Pisonia branches in its thousands but also uses wilted Pisonia leaves as the main building material in its excreta-cemented nests. If, as the bird enters or leaves the tree, it touches a ripening fruit cluster, the tenacious glue immediately sticks to the plumage and the individual fruits or the whole cluster break away very readily. The bird's wings may become glued to body or tail, or the tail may not be able to be spread, and the crippled bird flutters helplessly on the

Black Noddy crippled by a group of Pisonia fruits

Pisonia grandis (Pisonia) — male flowers

ground until it finally dies of starvation. Perhaps the decaying carcass provides a fertile site for the seedlings developing from the fruit it carried.

Although seedlings of Pisonia can occasionally be found, most propagation occurs through the rooting of fallen branches. Even a large log is likely to root wherever it touches the sand, and will soon produce a row of coppice shoots along its length. This shedding and rooting of branches provides a very effective means of advance into the surrounding community.

Family Olacaceae

Ximenia americana   Yellow Plum

Mistletoes are readily recognized as parasites, growing as they do on the branches of woody plants. Less obviously parasitic are those plants which attack the roots of other trees. One of these is *Ximenia americana*, a shrub or sprawling tree widespread along tropical coasts, with simple ovate-elliptical leaves often slightly notched at the apex. It is commonly, although not invariably, spiny.

Small, fragrant, cream or greenish-yellow flowers have four fairly firm petals which curl back revealing the dense hairs on the inner side. The plum-like fruits, about 2 cm broad, are edible when ripe and yellow or orange-red. When crushed, both green fruits and leaves have a strong odour of bitter almonds or benzaldehyde, an indication that prussic acid is being released. In spite of this, the young leaves have been used in India as a vegetable but only after cooking. The oily kernel also is edible, either raw or cooked, but it has been recommended that it be eaten only in small quantity. Oil extracted from the kernel has been used in soap- and candle-making and as a hairdressing.

Ximenia americana (Yellow Plum)

Family Oleaceae

Jasminum aemulum   Native Jasmine

Numerous species of *Jasminum* have been brought into cultivation as garden ornamentals, and *J. aemulum* could justifiably join this group. It is a scrambling shrub with simple, opposite leaves and small terminal or axillary groups

Jasminum aemulum (Native Jasmine)

of star-like white flowers about 2 cm across, with six to nine narrow, widely spreading, pointed petals which tend to bend backwards as they age. The delightful perfume characteristically associated with Jasmine is well developed in this species.

Jasminum racemosum   Climbing Jasmine

This species is readily distinguished from *Jasminum aemulum* by its twining habit and by its generally trifoliate leaves. The flowers are smaller than those of *J. aemulum* but still attractive.

Jasminum racemosum (Climbing Jasmine)

Family Orchidaceae

Dendrobium discolor   Golden Orchid

Orchids are generally thought of as tropical rainforest plants, so it is something of a surprise to find one growing on the shore within reach of the salt spray. The Golden Orchid occurs on rocks in such positions, but is not restricted to them, and may be seen in more protected situations or as an epiphyte on trees including mangroves. It is a robust plant, with numerous long pseudo-bulbs often 2–3 m long; these bear thick, flat ovate leaves sometimes with an apical notch. The flower sprays are long with numerous flowers about 5 cm in diameter; typically the blooms are brown and edged with golden yellow, with a touch of purple near the centre, but there is considerable variation, one form having pure yellow flowers. The spreading petals and sepals are rather narrow and strongly undulate so they do not lie flat; the species was formerly known as *Dendrobium undulatum*.

In spite of the complete protection of orchids in Queensland, many specimens of this handsome plant have been removed by collectors, so it is less common than it once was.

Dendrobium discolor (Golden Orchid)

Family Pandanaceae

Pandanus   Screw Pine

In Queensland, species of *Pandanus* are commonly known as Breadfruit because of the superficial resemblance of the large fruit to the true Breadfruit which Captain Bligh was carrying to the West Indies when his crew mutinied. The more widely known name of Screw Pine is derived from the spiralled arrangement of the leaves, most clearly seen in the overlapping, stem-clasping leaf bases. The generic name *Pandanus* is derived from the Malay word *pandan* used for this group of plants.

The tapered leaves, 0.5–2 m long, are crowded into a dense terminal crown and, as they fall, leave a smooth stem with faint, undulating horizontal bars. Leaves are prominently keeled and usually have the margins curved downwards so that they are roughly M-shaped in section. Along the margin and on the keel are closely placed forward-directed prickles, sharp as needles, which make it difficult to thrust a hand into the crown. Young leaves are coated with a waxy bloom often marked with a pattern of parallel scratches traced by the prickles of the adjacent leaf margin as the leaves separate.

In the thick litter beneath the tree can usually be found

Pandanus tectorius (Screw Pine)

some leaves from which the surface layers are flaking away to reveal a beautiful internal net of flattened longitudinal strands connected by numerous more delicate cross bars. This structure gives the leaf a resilience which makes it suitable material for weaving the sleeping mats which have been widely used by the native people of the Pacific area.

Where branching occurs, one branch has its base partly overgrown by that of its companion. Scattered over the older parts of the branches are numerous sharp, conical outgrowths, 2–4 mm high, actually roots with arrested development, which break through the surface layers lifting little flaps of tissue.

Characteristically, the trunk of *Pandanus* is buttressed by a group of stout prop roots which, unless injured, remain unbranched until they reach the sand. Each root tip, as it grows through the air, is protected by a laminated root cap sometimes the size of an egg cup. The prop roots emerge progressively higher on the trunk so that on a mature tree they may descend from a height of 2 m or more.

Pandanus tectorius
(Screw Pine)

The conical mass of prop roots enveloping the base of the trunk forms an effective shelter on some cays for the Bridled Tern, whose nest may be found on the ground beneath this natural tent. Within the cone of roots the trunk may narrow towards the base and, in some cases, may disappear at about ground level so that the tree is supported only by the roots.

The trunk has a relatively hard "casing", enclosing coarse fibrous strands embedded in softer tissue which decays

Pandanus tectorius (Screw Pine)

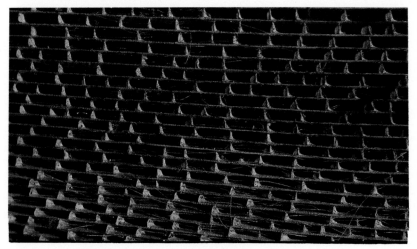

Pandanus tectorius (Screw Pine) – leaf skeleton

quickly after death. In India and Ceylon pieces of prop root with the ends frayed have been used as paint brushes.

Male and female flowers are borne on different trees. The very reduced male flowers, each consisting only of a group of stamens, are borne in a dense cream-coloured structure, 15 cm or more long, which has a remarkably strong fruity odour. Female flowers, also much reduced, are borne in an inconspicuous head and, after fertilization, develop into a pineapple-like fruit, orange when ripe, up to the size of a human head. This is composed of numerous wedge-shaped segments, or syncarps. The top of each syncarp is marked with five to twelve warts, the number corresponding to the number of flowers originally present in the group. Below each wart, encased in a woody shell, may be a single, elongate oily seed, which is edible but difficult to extract; however, many of the cavities are sterile. The fleshy, fibrous outer layer in the lower part of the ripe syncarps also is edible; a soft, sweet pulp can be chewed from between the fibres, but it often causes irritation to the throat unless boiled first.

The overlapping leaf bases retain water, in some cases for long enough for mosquito larvae to develop there. Water slowly seeping down the trunk from this reservoir provides a habitat for Blue-green Algae such as *Schizothrix friesii*. On leaning trunks this growth occurs as a prominent black streak down the lower side.

Several species occur in Queensland. A common one on sandy shores is *P. tectorius*.

See also in chapter 6, "Flotsam".

Family Passifloraceae

Passiflora foetida   Stinking Passion Flower,
                                    Love-in-a-mist Passion Flower

This naturalized passion flower with hairy, three-lobed leaves is more common than any of the three native species and may be found from the beaches to the margins of rain-forests, climbing over other plants to which it is firmly attached by tendrils.

It has two particularly distinctive features. One is the unpleasant foetid odour given off when the plant is bruised; the other is the group of three bracts, immediately beneath the flower, which are finely divided with each of the final hair-like branches ending in a sticky glandular tip; these bear some resemblance to similar structures in the garden Love-in-a-mist.

Beautiful white flowers open at night but the petals shrivel after the sun has been on them for about an hour. The fruit remains enclosed within the spidery bracts, eventually becoming yellow; at that stage it is edible, although the green fruit releases prussic acid when bruised.

Passiflora foetida (Stinking Passion Flower, Love-in-a-Mist Passion Flower)

Family Plumbaginaceae

Plumbago zeylanica   Native Leadwort

This species resembles a straggly plant of the blue-flowered *Plumbago capensis* of horticulture. Although a blue-flowered form of *P. zeylanica* occurs, most flowers seem to be white. The calyx bears short, sticky glandular hairs which sometimes trap small insects.

The roots are poisonous and their bruised bark is reported to raise blisters on the skin. However, it has been used medicinally in various countries. South African natives have used it in treating leprosy, in India it had the reputation of being able to cause abortion, while in Fiji a lotion prepared by boiling the roots in seawater has been applied to ringworms.

Plumbago zeylanica (Native Leadwort)

Family Poaceae (Gramineae)

To many people, grass is just grass and is highly uninteresting to the observer who prefers plants with showy flowers or perhaps edible fleshy fruits. Grass flowers are minute, without obvious petals, but surrounded by a pair of bracts and arranged in small groups known as spikelets of which there may be dozens or hundreds in an inflorescence. The ten thousand or more species in the family show a tremendous variety of form particularly in the structure and arrangement of the spikelets, and are fascinating for those who pay close attention.

There are about seven grasses common on the reef islands, all easily identified when in flower or fruit.

Cenchrus echinatus   Sand Burr, Mossman River Grass

This troublesome grass, native to tropical America, is best (or worst) recognized by its burr-like fruits. Each burr, enclosing one to several seeds, bears a ring of toughened spines and slender barbed bristles which provide a most effective means of dispersal. The burrs themselves are arranged in a short loose spike and are readily picked up by animal fur and

Cenchrus echinatus (Sand Burr, Mossman River Grass)

feathers, clothing and bare feet. *Cenchrus* has been widely spread by people through burrs attached to clothes and camping gear, and has probably been introduced to some islands by this means.

Eleusine indica   Crowsfoot Grass

A tough, strongly rooted plant, Crowsfoot Grass often grows as a flattened rosette of shining stems and leaves. The inflorescence has four or more spreading spikes from the apex and, commonly, another somewhat below this. It is an introduced weed, widespread in tropical and subtropical areas, the specific name meaning "of India". Stems of Crowsfoot Grass have had local use for hat-making in the Philippines.

Eleusine indica (Crowsfoot Grass)

Lepturus repens   Stalky Grass

Lepturus repens, at first glance, is uninteresting almost to the point of boredom, but like the other grasses repays detailed examination with an appreciation of its precise form and development. It is a common creeping grass of the cays, growing sometimes to high-water mark where it has a prostrate form. In sunlit glades away from the beach it is

Lepturus repens
(Stalky Grass)

more erect and tussocky. The long narrow leaves are rough to the touch on the upper surface and margins.

The flowering spike at first is narrow and stalk-like, as each spikelet is attached in a pit on the axis. As the flowers and then the seeds mature, the outer bract on each gradually bends outward to an angle of about 60°. When the seeds are ripe the axis breaks readily at the nodes, so that a short section of stem, less than a centimetre long, is shed, bearing one or two seeds with projecting bracts. These segments, when mature, float in sea water so may be dispersed in that way; slight teeth on the margins enable them to be carried by animals.

Spinifex hirsutus   Hairy Spinifex

This is the distinctive grey grass of the coastal dunes, and is commonly the earliest colonizer of newly deposited sand. Long, rapidly growing yellow runners carry tufts of leaves,

Spinifex hirsutus (Hairy Spinifex)

grey because of a closely pressed layer of colourless hairs. In the leaf are rows of specialized cells which collapse under dry conditions, causing the leaf to roll into a tight quill form; this cuts down further water loss and aids survival in the harsh conditions of the dune.

The plant tolerates well the partial burying which is a hazard of this environment and, in fact, seems to perform better there than in areas of non-shifting sand. This ability makes it of use in dune reclamation and protection programmes.

Male and female flowers occur usually on different plants in *Spinifex*. Male spikelets are produced mainly in terminal sprays; female inflorescences, which in some cases are actually bisexual, are more conspicuous, the radiating spikelets forming a bristling head 20 cm or more in diameter. When mature the entire spiny ball is shed and bowled along the beach by the wind until it meets an obstacle. If covered by blown sand, the seeds may germinate. However, the species spreads within a localized area mainly by the growth of its runners.

Sporobolus virginicus   Saltwater Couch, Sand Couch

Saltwater Couch is widespread in the warmer regions of the world; *virginicus* indicates that it was first described from

Sporobolus virginicus (Saltwater Couch, Sand Couch)

Virginia in North America. It is common in salt marshes on the mainland, often occurring on the salt flats behind mangrove swamps. The narrow inrolled leaves are stiff, erect and almost uncomfortably sharp to walk on; the flower spikes are of the rat's-tail type with very small individual spikelets producing minute black seeds which fall free of the husk and can be eaten by anyone with enough patience to gather them.

On the Reef islands *Sporobolus* occurs mainly in the marginal community of grasses and herbs near high-water mark.

Stenotaphrum micranthum   Beach Buffalo Grass

A grass mainly of shady places, this has relatively broad soft leaves, and in the vegetative stage shows considerable resemblance to *Thuarea involuta;* however, it lacks the

Stenotaphrum micranthum
(Beach Buffalo Grass)

velvety leaf surface of that species. It is easy to distinguish when in flower; the short branches, each bearing about four spikelets, are pressed against the axis of the inflorescence and are more or less embedded on either side in the "narrow ditch" which gives the name *Stenotaphrum*. The whole inflorescence is a narrow cylindrical spike.

At first sight the spike appears similar to that of *Lepturus* but can be distinguished by the clearly two-rowed arrangement of the spikelets in grooves on the axis. The shorter, broad leaves and generally softer appearance distinguish it when not in flower.

Thuarea involuta   Bird's-beak Grass

Among the first plants to stabilize newly deposited sand on the Reef islands is *Thuarea involuta*; its long creeping runners bear light green leaves, comparatively short and broad, and

Thuarea involuta (Bird's-beak Grass) — stages in development of inflorescence and fruit

densely coated with short hairs which give the leaves the softness of velvet.

The particularly interesting feature of *Thuarea* is its fruiting structure. At first, the flowering axis is enclosed and hidden by a slender boat-shaped sheath. Flowers are borne along only one side of a broad flattened axis and protrude from the sheath as they open. At the base are two bisexual flowers which are the first to open, each producing three anthers and a pair of white feathery stigmas. Then the five to seven male flowers above open in turn.

Usually before the flowering is complete the axis has started to bend out of its sheath. This bending is continued until the axis is folded down on itself, completely enclosing the two developing grains. At this stage the structure has something the appearance of a bird's head with a strong beak; to those with a different turn of imagination it has a superficial resemblance to the Greenhood Orchid (*Pterostylis*).

The fruit thus formed has a very hard water-tight covering formed from the axis of the spike; it is light and buoyant, with a large air space surrounding the two enclosed seeds, and air held in the rigid dead cells of the axis, so they are well adapted to dispersal by sea.

Family Portulacaceae

Portulaca oleracea   Pigweed, Purslane

A succulent plant, this is known to many home gardeners as a weed with rounded to wedge-shaped fleshy leaves and small yellow flowers. It is a native plant but is also widespread in many parts of the world; pioneers and others have found Pigweed a useful green vegetable substitute for spinach.

On some of the Reef islands Pigweed occurs in abundance, plants subject to salt spray often becoming very robust with thick reddish stems.

Portulaca oleracea (Pigweed, Purslane)

Family Rhamnaceae

Colubrina asiatica

Growing mainly in the northern part of the state, *Colubrina asiatica* is a common scrambling shrub of the strand, easily recognized by its strikingly shiny, more or less heart-shaped alternate leaves; these are rather thin, have scalloped margins, and possess two prominent lateral veins at the junction of leaf blade and stalk.

Small, inconspicuous greenish flowers are followed by clusters of up to six rounded, slightly three-lobed fruits, the basal third of the fruit sitting in the closely fitting cup formed by the calyx.

Like several other members of this family, this plant contains a saponin which is poisonous and will lather when agitated with water. This is no doubt the basis of its one-time use in Fiji in a hair wash which had the useful property of destroying vermin; in Samoa it has been used for washing mats. In the Philippines, a solution prepared from the leaves has been used to treat skin disease, and the fruits used as a fish poison.

Colubrina asiatica

Family Rubiaceae

Guettarda speciosa

Guettarda speciosa is a coarse shrub or small tree usually found close to the beach. The plant is easily recognized by its large, stiff, short-stalked opposite leaves, broadly ovate or almost round, with prominent yellowish veins and, in large specimens, up to about 30 cm long. On each side of the stem between the two leaves of a pair is a stipule, a small green flap which falls off soon after the leaves expand.

The white flowers, borne in tight clusters of approximately twenty, are about 1.5 cm across and have their petals united into a tube with from four to nine lobes. They are very sweetly scented but the plant is mainly a night flowerer and the perfume does not persist long into the day. Fruits are hard, depressed-globular, 2–3 cm broad, with a circular depression at the apex.

The perfume is sufficiently strong and attractive for it to have been exploited in India, where thin muslin was spread at night over the plant making contact with the flowers; perfume was absorbed by the dew-laden cloth and the scented solution wrung out in the morning. Described by an

Guettarda speciosa

Indian writer as deliciously fragrant, the flowers are popular in garlands and as hair ornaments.

Although it is not exploited in Australia, the timber is durable and has been used in Fiji for house stumps.

See also in chapter 6, "Flotsam".

Morinda citrifolia   Cheese Fruit

The large, elliptical, bright green glossy leaves of this small northern tree are up to 30 cm long. At the junction of each of the principal lateral veins with the midrib there is a small tuft of hairs, and on the stem between each pair of leaves is a pair of stipules, small flaps of tissue which fall off fairly early. In the absence of flowers and fruits this species is easily distinguished from *Guettarda speciosa* by the absence of hairs on the under leaf surface other than at the vein junctions.

The white flowers are united into groups of fifty or so and open a few at a time. The composite fruit arising from this group is irregularly egg-shaped, up to about 10 cm long, and cream-coloured and soft when ripe. Although it is edible, a revolting odour of very rotten cheese, and a flavour to match, leads to a marked lack of demand for the fruit.

The bark and leaves have been used in Tahiti and New Caledonia as a tonic and to reduce fever. In South-East Asia,

Morinda citrifolia (Cheese Fruit)

before the advent of synthetic dyes, a yellow dye was extracted from the roots and used for the well-known batik method of dyeing cloth.

Myrmecodia beccarii   Ant Plant

One of the plant oddities of moist coastal tropics of eastern Australia is the Ant Plant. These specialized plants are found as epiphytes mainly on *Melaleuca viridiflora* (Broad-leaved Tea-tree) in swampy land near the sea, but may grow also on associated trees and on mangroves. Most of the stem is a grey-brown, irregular tuberous structure, 30 cm across in larger plants, commonly armed with small prickles, inconspicuous to the eye but not to the fingers. Protruding from the tuber are one or more stumpy, leafy branches, very knobbly because of the presence of large, deeply depressed leaf scars. Small white flowers are borne on these knobbly branches. The tuber is penetrated by a labyrinth of canals

Myrmecodia beccarii
(Ant Plant)

occupied by aggressive small ants which stream out from small holes to repel the cause of any disturbance to their refuge.

Randia fitzalanii   Papajarin

A small tree with an open canopy, *Randia fitzalanii* has firm-textured leaves 15 cm or more in length, glossy dark green

Randia fitzalanii (Papajarin)

Randia fitzalanii (Papajarin)

with pale veins, broad at the apex and tapering to a short stalk.

Very fragrant gardenia-scented white flowers in loose clusters at the ends of the branches make the tree most attractive. The flowers have a short broad tube and a flat face of five slightly overlapping petals which are remarkably tough in texture; individual flowers are about 3 cm in diameter. Although all the flowers have apparent stamens and ovaries, not all are functional so that in effect the trees are either male or female.

Large green fruit, becoming yellow when ripe, are distinctive; before maturing they are about the size and colour of a small Granny Smith apple, although slightly elongate and with the stalk and flower remains not sunken as they are in an apple.

Although common along tropical shores, the trees are not restricted to them and occur frequently in rainforests.

Timonius timon

Although apparently not occurring on the cays, this small tree is very common on some of the continental shelf islands such as those of the Whitsunday area. Its opposite leaves, mostly 6–10 cm long, are elliptical and drawn out at the apex to a sharp point. The undersurface is sparsely hairy, and at

Timonius timon – fruits and female flower

the junctions of the prominently raised veins are domatia, small pouch-like structures evident on the underside as a tuft of hairs and opening to the upper surface by a small pore. Particularly in spring, many of the leaves turn pink or red before falling, and the trees are then readily recognized from a distance. The white fleshy flowers, 1.5–2 cm across, are unisexual, the male and female flowers being borne on different trees. Male flowers occur in small groups of up to seven in the leaf axils; the five petals are marked with fleshy scales and support five anthers. Female flowers are borne singly in the axils; they have ten petals each with a fleshy ridge on the upper side, ten rudimentary stamens and an ovary which develops into a globose fruit, up to about 1.5 cm across, crowned by the persistent calyx.

Family Sapindaceae

Cupaniopsis anacardioides   Cupania Tree, Tuckeroo

The Cupania Tree is an important constituent of the poorly developed rainforest sometimes found on sand close to the shore. Its coarse pinnate leaves have six to ten leaflets, often notched at the apex. As in many members of the family there is a prominent swelling at the base of the leaf stalk. Flowers are inconspicuous but are followed by prominent clusters of hard, yellow three-lobed fruits. At maturity, each splits widely into three valves revealing three erect seeds enveloped in a thin, orange-red fleshy layer, sometimes not quite complete so that a small patch of black seed-coat shows through. After the seeds are shed the fruits fall, often coming to rest with the short and now hardened stalk directed upwards and very uncomfortable to bare feet.

Cupaniopsis anacardioides (Cupania Tree)

Family Sapotaceae

Mimusops elengi   Tanjong Tree

Tanjong Trees form small shapely specimens with rounded crowns. The leaves, borne alternately on rusty hairy twigs, have an elliptical leaf blade 5–10 cm long, often with an undulate margin. Highly perfumed star-shaped flowers, a little over one centimetre across, are borne in the leaf axils; there are eight acute sepals, and eight two-lobed white petals which fall from spent flowers as a ring. When ripe the fruits are orange-red, more or less globose, about 1.5 cm broad, and have an edible, floury flesh surrounding the single large seed.

Mimusops elengi (Tanjong Tree)

Because of their persistent fragrance and ring-shaped form, the fallen petals are often strung into garlands in India and South-East Asia. They are also sometimes used for stuffing pillows and are infused to make a perfumed cosmetic water. The plant has a wide variety of medicinal uses in South-East Asia; among them are the use of crushed or boiled leaves for external application in the case of headaches, and the use of leaves and flowers to prepare a tonic for treatment of fever and diarrhoea.

Planchonella obovata

Although it is one of the less distinctive trees close to the shore, *Planchonella obovata* is a very common species in some places, such as on Green Island. A flow of milky latex from damaged bark is one clue to its identity. The leaves, almost opposite, are mostly obovate in outline and very variable in size, the leaf blade being mostly 8–18 cm long. Small greenish-cream flowers, opening flat, are densely crowded in leaf axils and produce copious nectar, sometimes in such quantity that rocks beneath the tree are moistened by the dripping solution. The fruits are small, elongate and purplish.

Planchonella obovata

Pouteria sericea   Mongo

The Mongo can be a small shapely tree but more often is seen as a weather-beaten or wind-sheared specimen commonly reduced to shrub form, clinging tenaciously to crevices on rocky headlands. Its alternate, leathery, broadly elliptical leaves, 3-6 cm long, have a dense coating of silky, silvery or silvery-brown hairs on the underside, often with darker flecks here and there imparting an almost dirty appearance.

Flowers occur singly or in small groups in the leaf axils;

Pouteria sericea (Mongo)

Pouteria sericea (Mongo)

they have a tubular, five-lobed yellow-green corolla and shorter rusty-brown calyx lobes. The purple-black fruit, about olive size, has a palatable flesh surrounding the single ellipsoid stone.

Family Solanaceae

Solanum americanum   Black Nightshade

Black Nightshade is an erect herb familiar to many home gardeners as a minor weed. Small, white star-like flowers, with prominent yellow anthers in a central group, are borne in a cluster of three to nine on a common stalk. Fruit are 6–8 mm across, round, glossy black when ripe, and edible at this stage in spite of the common name Deadly Nightshade which is sometimes erroneously applied to this species.

Solanum americanum (Black Nightshade)

Family Surianaceae

Suriana maritima

This is a twiggy shrub sometimes forming extensive thickets
1–2 m high. Its narrow, crowded, pale green leaves are
2–3.5 cm long, and not more than 5 mm across their broader
upper part. Leaves and young stems are densely clothed with
fine hairs.

The flowers are star-shaped, about 1 cm across, with five
bright-yellow petals; however they are not conspicuous as
they are surrounded by the pale foliage, which frequently has
yellowish leaves among it, and the persistent green sepals are
of about the same length as the petals. Flowers are produced
in short sprays but open only one at a time.

Although not strikingly individual in appearance, this plant
is relatively distinctive on some of the cays, its narrow,
almost heath-like foliage providing a contrast to the generally
broad-leaved vegetation.

Suriana maritima

Family Tiliaceae

Triumfetta rhomboidea   Chinese Burr

Like many other plants with fruits which are easily attached to clothing or animal fur, Chinese Burr has become a widespread and unwelcome plant of tropical regions. It is a small shrub with alternate toothed leaves of variable form but usually with three sharply pointed lobes. A few of the marginal teeth close to the leaf stalk often produce glistening droplets of sticky fluid; star-shaped hairs occur on the underside. The small yellow flowers, in close clusters, usually open about midday, the five greenish-yellow sepals and five yellow petals opening widely. The less attractive fruits which follow are rounded burrs densely covered with spines, each tipped with a minute but effective hook.

The plant is a pest in Australia, but in parts of Africa and India a jute substitute has been prepared from the fibrous bark, and strips of the bark have sometimes been used for making ropes. Although reported to be an emergency green vegetable, its toughness and somewhat pungent flavour make it one of the species to be used only as a last resort.

A second species of *Triumfetta* is the Bingil Burr, *T. procumbens*, a prostrate plant whose toothed three-lobed leaves

Triumfetta rhomboidea (Chinese Burr)

Triumfetta procumbens (Bingil Burr)

are clothed on both surfaces with small, hard, three-branched recurved hairs which make them thick and rough to the touch. The yellow flowers are followed by rounded burrs, about 15 mm in diameter, covered densely with coarse conical spines.

Family Ulmaceae

Celtis paniculata   Native Elm

Celtis paniculata is a smooth-barked tree of slender outline with the branchlets often drooping. The dark-green leaves, up to 10 cm long and about twice as long as broad, are slightly sickle-shaped and asymmetrical at the base. A pair of prominent lateral veins arise where the leaf blade joins its stalk.

Loosely branched clusters of small cream flowers are followed by small black fruits about 1 cm long.

Celtis paniculata (Native Elm)

Family Urticaceae

Pipturus argenteus   Native Mulberry

A small tree of the nettle family, *Pipturus argenteus* has leaves similar to those of a stinging nettle in shape, but lacking the stinging hairs; the underside of the leaves, and the young stems, are whitish with closely pressed hairs. Leaf stalks are relatively long and often pink.

Male and female flowers are carried on separate trees; both are small and fairly inconspicuous. Small globular clusters of female flowers develop into a rounded white compound fruit about 6 mm across; this is fleshy and pleasant to eat.

As with many other members of this family, the inner bark is a source of strong fibres; these have been used in Samoa to make fishing nets.

Pipturus argenteus (Native Mulberry)

Family Verbenaceae

Clerodendrum inerme   Sorcerer's Flower

On many tropical strands of the Malaysian-Pacific area, *Clerodendrum inerme* is a common sprawling and scrambling shrub. Vegetatively it is an uninteresting-looking plant, its slightly fleshy ovate-elliptical leaves, in pairs or threes, having no particularly distinctive feature. However, its white flowers are attractive; the lower parts of the petals are united to form a slender tube 2–3 cm long, with five expanded lobes at the apex. Four purple-red stamens protrude well beyond the petals. Species of *Clerodendrum* are often pollinated by butterflies whose long proboscis can reach the nectar at the base of the tube. The fruits of this species are commonly distorted following attack by a gall-inducing insect.

In Guam, the leaves have been used as a poultice for bruises, and the bitter roots in the treatment of fever – possibly the efficacy of quinine in treating malaria is responsible for a common belief that bitter plants are likely to be useful in reducing fever.

Some of the species of *Clerodendrum* were believed by Indian and Malaysian people to have magical properties; in Malaysia, *Clerodendrum* flowers have been used as a magical

Clerodendrum inerme (Sorcerer's Flower)

assistance in setting traps for animals, the projecting stamens suggesting beckoning arms. Fruits of *C. inerme* were regarded by the sailors of Macassar as useful for treating people poisoned by fish or crabs; in Java they were used for cases of dysentery.

Premna corymbosa

This strand shrub or small tree is found only in the northern part of the state. Its shiny, broadly elliptical to heart-shaped, opposite leaves are mostly 6–22 cm long. A much-branched flat-topped cluster of small inconspicuous flowers terminates the branch. Fruits are round, cream at first but turning black, and are only 5 mm across; when shed, they leave the persistent calyx as a little saucer on the plant.

The pith of the stem has a peculiar form, being longitudinally ribbed with approximately fourteen flanges surrounding the central hollow and at intervals of about 5 mm supporting thin horizontal discs. Aborigines used the timber for fire sticks.

Premna corymbosa

Stachytarpheta jamaicensis   Blue Snakeweed

A tall herb with four-angled purple stems and opposite toothed leaves showing a purple tinge in the lower part of the midrib, Blue Snakeweed occurs in the northern islands and

Stachytarpheta jamaicensis
(Blue Snakeweed)

coastal parts of Queensland as a roadside and trackside plant.

The striking feature is the long snake-like flower spike, about 30 cm long but only a few millimetres broad; the pattern on the spike is made by closely pressed bracts. Small purple-blue flowers open in succession, so at any one time there may be one or two open blooms on the spike.

Blue Snakeweed has been used medicinally in India for a variety of ailments including ulcers of several kinds and dysentery. In Brazil, dried leaves of this species have been used as an adulterant in tea, and have been exported as Brazilian Tea.

A very similar species, *Stachytarpheta urticifolia* (Purple Snakeweed), sometimes growing with *S. jamaicensis*, is distinguished from the latter by its more distinctly purple flowers and by some bulging up of the leaf tissue between the veins.

Vitex negundo

Vitex negundo is a sparse shrub with four-angled stems bearing opposite, aromatic leaves with three to five radiating leaflets, the central one usually distinctly stalked. Upper leaf surfaces are greyish, undersurfaces almost white, because of different densities of fine hairs on the two sides. Attractive but small blue-purple, two-lipped flowers are borne mainly in terminal sprays in which usually only a few flowers are open at any one time.

The plant is an important one in Indian medicine, leaves and roots being used to treat a wide variety of complaints including worms, rheumatism, boils and dysentery. Leaves are smoked to give relief from headache and catarrh.

Vitex negundo

Vitex ovata   Creeping Vitex
(V. trifolia var. *simplicifolia)*

Unlike *Vitex negundo* this shrub is prostrate, the main stems running across the sand often for a couple of metres, rooting here and there, sometimes partly buried, and producing only very short erect shoots. Strongly aromatic leaves are densely hairy. The purple-blue, two-lipped flowers are a little longer than those of *V. negundo* and the sprays more compact.

Vitex ovata (Creeping Vitex)

Overall it is an attractive and unusual plant and has had some use as a garden ornamental over the last few years.

Family Zygophyllaceae

Tribulus cistoides   Bull's Head

Visitors to the Reef islands frequently become aware of this species, either by seeing its strikingly bright yellow flowers or by standing on its strikingly prickly fruits.

It is a spreading herb with prostrate stems radiating from a deeply penetrating root. In non-flowering parts the finely hairy pinnate leaves are usually alternate, but in flowering parts usually opposite with one leaf of each pair characteristically smaller than the other. Flowers are borne singly in the axil of the smaller leaf, or if there should be only one leaf, then opposite it.

The flower is a bright, clear yellow, 2–3 cm across and broadly cup-shaped. There are ten stamens which shed their pollen into the base of the flower. By early afternoon the flowers are past their prime, and in many the petals have rolled upwards and inwards so that they appear as five narrow quills, giving the nearly spent flower the form of a star.

The fruit is a rough, deeply ribbed structure of up to five lobes, each with four robust prickles pointing in different directions. On drying, the lobes separate as wedge-shaped

Tribulus cistoides (Bull's Head)

segments which come to rest nearly always with one of the larger prickles directed upwards.

A small butterfly, the Dark Grass-blue (*Zizeeria karsandra*), can often be seen fluttering around plants of *Tribulus cistoides*.

5   *Flowering plants in the sea*

An overwhelming number of the several thousand species of marine plants are algae, but there are two groups of flowering plants, the mangroves and the sea-grasses, which have invaded the sea. In spite of the small number of species involved, these plants, because of their size and vigorous development in intertidal and shallow waters, are a conspicuous and important part of the marine vegetation of tropical coasts.

Mangroves

Mangroves are a group of flowering shrubs and trees which occupy saline intertidal sand and mud. The plants are related ecologically rather than botanically, fifteen families of diverse origin having contributed species to the mangroves of Australian shores.

By the standards of normal plant growth the habitat occupied by mangroves is one which presents major difficulties. The substrate is relatively unstable but, more important, it is often devoid of free oxygen, which roots require for their respiration. Twice a day most adult mangroves experience partial submersion while many seedlings experience total submersion. The water on which the plants depend is saline and would quickly kill most other flowering plants. Nevertheless, mangroves have developed various structural and physiological characters which fit them for this unusual habitat.

Most striking of the structural specializations are the root modifications which provide a large surface area well supplied with lenticels – these are small pores, partly blocked by loose cork cells, which allow gas exchange between the atmosphere and internal air passages leading to the buried roots. Particularly conspicuous among these highly modified roots are the stilt roots of *Rhizophora* and the pneumatophores of *Avicennia*.

All the mangroves are efficient at excluding salt from the water taken up by the roots. Some, such as species of *Rhizophora*, are particularly efficient and take up no more than is sufficient to give the tissues a slightly salty taste when chewed. Others, such as *Aegiceras corniculatum*, are not quite such efficient salt excluders, but they do not accumulate salt to damaging levels because they excrete, through glands on the leaf, most of the small amount of salt which the roots let through.

Another modification found in some mangroves, and whose benefit to the plant is not wholly clear, is the development of vivipary. This is the condition in which the seed germinates without any period of dormancy while still within the fruit, and eventually leaves the tree as a well-developed seedling.

In Australia, mangroves have been relatively little used by people. They were a minor source of tannin, of oyster stakes and, in the early days, of barilla, an alkaline ash used for making soap; the Aborigines have used seeds and seedlings of some of them for food. There has been a widespread view that mangroves are mosquito and midge infested swamps best filled in and put to some useful purpose. As a consequence of this view, large areas of Australian mangroves have been lost. More recently, it has been realized that mangroves, particularly through the nutrients they provide by leaf shedding, make a major contribution to coastal marine food chains and have an importance well beyond their immediate vicinity. For example, it has been shown that most of the sport and commercial fish in the Gulf of Mexico are linked to food chains originating in mangrove detritus. Evidence so far gathered suggests that mangroves have a similar importance in Australia. Opinion is slowly swinging towards a favourable view of this extremely interesting group of plants.

Family Acanthaceae

Acanthus ilicifolius   Holly-leaved Mangrove

A sparsely branched shrub, *Acanthus ilicifolius* grows along the landward margin of the mangrove community. The plants are not very woody; some of the stems, especially those produced at an angle, have thick, spongy aerial roots produced at the nodes.

The scientific name is appropriate; *acanthus* means "a thorn" and *ilicifolius* indicates "holly-leaved". Each of the opposite leaves has a pair of needle-like spines about 5 mm long at the base, and the undulate leaf margin is usually also well armed with widely spaced sharp teeth. The leaves are elongate-elliptical, up to 12 cm long; they bear salt glands on their upper surface.

Pale-blue flowers are produced in four rows in terminal

Acanthus ilicifolius
(Holly-leaved Mangrove)

spikes, each flower having a distinct bract beneath; the petals are united into a broad-spreading lip 2.5 cm long, lobed at the end. The fruits are green, square-cylindrical, about 3 by 1 cm; each is topped with a wiry brown style.

The leaves have been used medicinally in Indonesia as poultices for wounds from poisoned arrows, and for various pains. In some parts of South-East Asia the leaves are chewed as a tobacco when nothing better is available, which presumably would not be often, as the spines would be very uncomfortable.

Family Caesalpiniaceae

Cynometra iripa   Wrinkle-pod Mangrove
(*C. ramiflora* var. *bijuga*)

This small mangrove with branches at irregular angles is a straggly, untidy shrub found at the landward edge of the mangrove forest. Its distinctive leaves are pinnate and shortly stalked. The leaflets of the upper pair are always appreciably larger than those of the lower pair. All are notched at the apex, and are very uneven-sided at the base where there is a very short, wrinkled stalk.

The unusual fruits are short, flattened, deeply wrinkled pods ending in a beak-like point and suggesting the head of a very old, bald parrot.

In India, leprosy and scabies have been treated with a lotion prepared from the leaves and with oil extracted from the seeds.

See also in chapter 6, "Flotsam".

Cynometra iripa (Wrinkle-pod Mangrove)

Family Combretaceae

Lumnitzera littorea   Red-flowered Black Mangrove

The distinctive root modification in *Lumnitzera littorea* is a knee root, appearing above the mud as a springy loop a few

Lumnitzera littorea (Red-flowered Black Mangrove)

Lumnitzera racemosa
(White-flowered Black Mangrove)

centimetres across, which does not become massive and knobbly as does the knee root in *Bruguiera*. The rather fleshy, alternate leaves are broadest in their upper part, often slightly notched at their rounded apex, and on the underside just behind the apex bear a small gland-like structure. The flowers, with five pillar-box red petals and ten projecting stamens, are borne in decorative terminal clusters.

L. racemosa (White-flowered Black Mangrove) has similar leaves but is without knee roots and is less showy, with white flowers in clusters in the leaf axils.

Family Euphorbiaceae

Excoecaria agallocha   Milky Mangrove, Blind-your-eye

Milky Mangrove is a neat, small tree with thick, shiny, alternate elliptical leaves about 5 cm long. As the leaves age they turn orange-red, and presence of some coloured leaves on the tree can be used to distinguish this species from other mangroves. A further characteristic is the presence of a pair of small glands, just visible to the naked eye, on the back of the leaf where the blade joins the stalk.

Care should be taken in handling this plant. Broken tissues exude a caustic milky latex which is able to cause temporary blindness if splashed in the eye. It can cause severe irritation to the skin, although the reaction of individuals varies; even inhalation of the vapour is reported to have caused headaches and throat irritation. This caustic latex has been used in native medicine as a drastic treatment for persistent ulcers, both in Australia and elsewhere.

Male and female flowers are borne on separate trees. Individually small, the male flowers are produced in cone-like structures, the females in short sprays.

Although typically a mangrove, this species is not infrequently found in the sandy intertidal zone away from the mud generally associated with a mangrove swamp.

Excoecaria agallocha (Milky Mangrove, Blind-your-eye)

Family Meliaceae

Xylocarpus granatum   Cannonball Tree

Xylocarpus granatum is one of the few mangroves with pinnate leaves, each leaf having usually four or six opposite leaflets. Its axillary sprays of small pinkish flowers, with generally four petals and with the eight stamens united into an urn-like structure, are not showy, but the fruits which eventually develop are spectacular, being globose green structures up to 12 cm across, hanging well clear of the foliage, and well justifying the common name. Within the tough, leathery rind are a dozen or more angular, pale-pink, pithy seeds fitting neatly together like a three-dimensional puzzle.

The tree has smooth bark, mottled due to its shedding in flakes. At the base it is strongly buttressed, with the buttresses snaking out from the trunk as undulate emergent roots, reminiscent of illustrations of sea-serpents.

The timber is similar to that of the well-known Red Cedar, another member of this family, but is available only in small sizes.

Xylocarpus granatum (Cannonball Tree)

A second species of the genus, *X. australasicum* (Cedar Mangrove) is readily distinguished from the preceding species by its deciduous nature and by producing numerous woody pneumatophores, often slightly flattened, up to 40 cm high.

See also in chapter 6, "Flotsam".

Family Myrsinaceae

Aegiceras corniculatum   River Mangrove

Although it sometimes attains the size of a small tree, the River Mangrove is usually a shrub of head height or less. It tolerates a wide range of salinities and, as its common name suggests, is the mangrove found furthest upriver although still within tidal regions. Not restricted to this habitat, it occurs also in the landward zone of mangroves along the shore.

The shrubs have alternate glossy leaves, elliptical with a rounded apex. There are glands on the leaves which excrete salt solution to such an extent that, except after rain, the upper surface bears a thin coating of salt crystals. Often there is also a dark film of sooty mould on the surface; this fungus is not a parasite on the mangrove, but is living on secretions from the leaf surface. The plants have a shallow, horizontal root system, but no obvious root modification allowing for aeration.

Sweetly scented flowers are produced in umbels – clusters with stalks radiating from a common point, mainly in leaf axils. Sharp-pointed conical buds open into small, white five-petalled flowers. The plants are viviparous and the fruits,

Aegiceras corniculatum (River Mangrove)

Aegiceras corniculatum (River Mangrove)

when ready for shedding, are about 3 cm long and curved like little horns, which is the meaning of *corniculatum*.

The bark has been used as a fish poison in South-East Asia. See also in chapter 6, "Flotsam".

Family Myrtaceae

Osbornia octodonta   Myrtle Mangrove

This very large family has contributed only one species to the mangroves, and *Osbornia octodonta* is the only mangrove with leaves dotted with minute translucent oil glands, a character of most members of the Myrtaceae. The plant reaches the stature of a small tree up to about 5 m high, and the usually crooked trunks are clothed with fibrous, stringy bark, reddish brown in colour but sometimes with the outer layers bleached to a pale grey-brown. Twigs are prominently four-angled, reddish at first, and bear opposite leaves in four distinct rows. The leaves are 3–4 cm long with the apices rounded and usually notched, and with the midrib reddish in the lower part. Since the leaves are often held more or less parallel to the stem it is mainly the undersurfaces which are presented to view. Small, cream, bell-shaped flowers are borne in the leaf axils either singly or in twos or threes; they have eight hairy calyx lobes but no petals.

The wood is very durable and apparently makes good firewood, since many of the specimens growing on Low Isles were once cut for fuel by the crews of luggers searching for trochus shell. In the Philippines, the bark has been used for caulking boats. The aromatic oil from crushed leaves, rubbed on the skin, is believed to act as an insect repellent.

Osbornia octodonta (Myrtle Mangrove)

Family Plumbaginaceae

Aegialitis annulata   Club Mangrove

This is probably the smallest of the Australian mangroves, often no more than a metre high; it has a tendency to occur in stony areas rather than soft mud. The trunk is distinctly broadened towards the base and so is roughly club-shaped. Leaf blades are diamond-elliptical, 3–7 cm long, and have an appreciably longer leaf stalk, its lower part prominently winged and stem-clasping. Numerous small pits on the upper surface are salt glands through which excess salt is excreted. The prominent rings left on the stem when the leaves fall justify the specific epithet *annulata*. Flowers are borne in terminal sprays. The five sepals are united to form a prominently ridged tube, from the apex of which spread five white petal lobes about 4 mm long.

Aegialitis annulata (Club Mangrove)

Family Pteridaceae

Acrostichum speciosum   Mangrove Fern

Ferns are sometimes found as epiphytes on mangroves, but *Acrostichum* is unusual in growing in the soil in mangrove swamps. It is not, in the strict sense, a mangrove, as it is commonly accepted that only woody intertidal plants are classed as such.

There are two species of *Acrostichum* along the Queensland coast, *A. speciosum* being the better known. It has a short horizontal stem with erect, leathery, pinnate fronds up to 1.5 m tall. Fertile fronds are distinctive with the upper leaflets completely coated on their undersurface with a rusty brown layer of sporangia, velvety in appearance but not in texture.

The Mangrove Fern occurs in association with mangroves along the length of the eastern Queensland coast and beyond. A similar species, with fronds at least twice as long and with the apices of sterile leaflets rounded rather than drawn to a point, is *A. aureum*; this is restricted in Australia to the far north coast of Queensland.

Stems of both species have been used as food, after roasting, by the Aborigines. In some islands of the South Pacific the fronds have been threaded to make thatch.

Acrostichum speciosum (Mangrove Fern)

Family Rhizophoraceae

Bruguiera gymnorhiza   Orange Mangrove

This mangrove is a medium-sized tree with opposite, leathery leaves 15–20 cm long, tipped by a slender point. As in species of *Rhizophora* and *Ceriops*, paired stipules form a slender conical sheath enclosing the next leaf, and, when it falls, leaving a prominent scar encircling the stem. The flowers are borne singly in the leaf axils and have a distinctive, often red, rigid, bell-shaped calyx with ten to thirteen claw-like lobes about 2 cm long. Vivipary is well developed, and eventually a cigar-like hypocotyl protrudes from between the calyx lobes, finally falling as a well-developed seedling with a small conical shoot at the upper end.

The bases of old trunks are often enlarged and may bear a few aerial roots but there are no distinct plank buttresses.

Bruguiera gymnorhiza
(Orange Mangrove)

Roots growing horizontally through the substrate loop above the surface at intervals, eventually thickening to form knobbly excrescences protruding up to 15 cm above the mud. These knee roots are provided with large lenticels, and almost certainly are involved in aeration of the buried parts of the root system.

Bruguiera exaristata can be distingushed from *B. gymnorhiza* by having only eight to ten calyx lobes and by the ribbing of the undivided part of the calyx and of the protruding hypocotyl.

Bark of species of *Bruguiera* has a high tannin content and has been used in South-East Asia for tanning hides; in Australia it seems to have been used mainly for tanning fishing nets in the days when these were made from cotton. Aborigines have used the hypocotyl for food after extensive preparation which removed much of the tannin.

See also in chapter 6, "Flotsam".

Ceriops tagal   Yellow Mangrove

This distinctive mangrove can often be recognized from some distance, even from the air, by the yellowish green of the leaves. Its other distinguishing feature is the strongly buttressed base. The lower trunk and the branched buttresses are marked with lenticels, large corky pustules important for aeration of the internal tissues. Weathered bases of *Ceriops*, collected as driftwood, are popular for ornamental purposes. Although usually shrubby, specimens sometimes reach the size of a small tree.

The leaves are opposite and shiny, with a round apex, and tend to stand erect. Small flowers have five sharply pointed, sometimes recurved sepals and white petals notched at the apex, where there are three bristles. The hypocotyl produced viviparously as in *Rhizophora* is up to about 20 cm long, about pencil thickness but broader in the apical part. There are two varieties of the species: var. *australis* has a smooth hypocotyl and flowers borne in pairs, while the less widespread var. *tagal* has a broadly ribbed hypocotyl and flowers in clusters.

The leaves and bark are rich in tannin; they are not much used in tanning but have been used in Asia for toughening fishing lines and nets. This plant is one of the sources of tradi-

Ceriops tagal (Yellow Mangrove)

Ceriops tagal (Yellow Mangrove)

tional dyes for batik, and used in combination with indigo can give a variety of colours from black to purple. Medicinally the tannin has been used as a astringent for haemorrhages and ulcers. The wood is hard and durable, suitable for building boat knees, and is a good-quality fuel.

Another species, *C. decandra*, has clustered flowers, a ribbed hypocotyl and pointed calyx lobes emerging part way along the fruit rather than at the base. The small petals have fringed lobes. This species has a limited distribution in Queensland, around Cairns and the Herbert River.

See also in chapter 6, "Flotsam".

Rhizophora stylosa   Spider Mangrove, Stilt Mangrove

Probably the most spectacular of all the mangroves are the species of *Rhizophora* with their distinctive prop roots arising from the trunk like flying buttresses, the series of root branches from them looping out over the mud. Similar roots often descend from the lower branches. When the aerial roots of adjacent trees intermingle they form a barrier which can be traversed only with the greatest difficulty. The appearance of these roots suggests that their function is concerned with supporting the tree in the soft, unstable substrate, but almost certainly their more important function is to provide a

Rhizophora stylosa (Spider Mangrove, Stilt Mangrove)

Rhizophora stylosa (Spider Mangrove, Stilt Mangrove)

means of aerating the roots beneath the mud; the aerial roots provide a large surface area over which lenticels are scattered and through which the air enters and then passes along well-developed channels to the submerged roots.

Shoot apices are conical, with a pair of stipules sheathing the next pair of leaves to expand. The opposite leaves are leathery, rather brittle and marked on the undersurface with dark-brown specks which are similar to small lenticels. Flowers are borne in axillary groups in which the axis undergoes forking usually two to four times so that generally four or more flowers occur in the group. There are four leathery, cream calyx lobes which persist in the fruit, four hair-fringed petals, eight almost stalkless anthers, and a central style a little shorter than the petals. The single seed which matures germinates within the tough pear-shaped fruit and the conical first root breaks through its apex. Eventually there protrudes from the fruit a pointed, slightly club-shaped structure 30–50 cm long, 1.5–2 cm wide. This structure eventually falls from the fruit as a well-developed seedling, the embryonic root at one end, a small conical shoot at the other, and in the intermediate region, the hypocotyl or transitional structure, a large storehouse of nutrients to see the seedling through a period of often several weeks until it becomes established. Being "bottom heavy", the seedling, when it leaves the parent, sometimes spears into the mud below,

Rhizophora stylosa, fringing stream on Hinchinbrook Island

planting itself. However, such seedlings have stiff competition from the parent tree. Seedlings which float away and eventually come to rest on a suitable mud bank develop numerous roots from the lower end; when once attached, differential growth of the hypocotyl leads to the structure erecting itself, although it is often left with a curve.

R. stylosa is the most common and widely distributed species in eastern Australia, extending from Cape York into northern New South Wales, but three other species occur in Queensland. *R. mucronata* differs from *R. stylosa* in lacking a distinct style and in having usually only one or two flowers in a group. The other two species lack the brown specks which characterize the under leaf surface of the preceding species, and have usually more than eight stamens; *R. apiculata* has almost hairless petals while those of *R. lamarckii* have hairy margins; the latter species only rarely produces mature fruits and seedlings, and is thought to be a hybrid between *R. stylosa* and *R. apiculata.*

See also in chapter 6, "Flotsam".

Family Rubiaceae

Scyphiphora hydrophylacea   Yamstick Mangrove

Shrubs of this species are generally found near the landward edge of mangrove communities where they are flooded only at spring tides. They are readily recognized by the opposite, shiny leaves, rounded at the apex and broadest above the mid--point, and by the small triangular flap of tissue, the stipule, which occurs between the leaf stalks on each side of the stem. Young shoots are often distinctly sticky. The white flowers, in small axillary groups, are tubular with four or five spreading petals and a protruding pink style forking near its apex. As the common name implies, the wood, which is dark brown and very hard, was used by the Aborigines for making yam sticks.

Scyphiphora hydrophylacea (Yamstick Mangrove)

Family Sonneratiaceae

Sonneratia alba   Pornupan

This species is a northern one extending southwards to the
Whitsunday area. The opposite, broadly elliptical leaves are
fleshy but brittle, snapping very readily. Its flowers make it
probably the most handsome of the Queensland mangroves.
The broadly cylindrical buds open to allow a mass of stamens
to expand into a decorative white brush 4 cm long. These
stamens survive only a few hours but even after they fall
what remains of the flower is still attractive; the inner faces
of the six or seven broadly spreading, triangular calyx lobes
are coloured from creamy green near the tips to deep purple-
pink at the base. Flattened fruits are topped with the remains
of the style.

The mangrove has breathing roots, or pneumatophores,
similar to those of the more common *Avicennia* but they are
much more robust structures, elongate-conical, and occasionally up to 1 m high.

No use seems to have been made of the species in Australia
but in India and South-East Asia both leaves and fruits have
been an item of food. In the Philippines the acid fruit has
been used for preparing vinegar while the pneumatophores
have been used for soles of shoes.

Sonneratia alba (Pornupan)

Family Sterculiaceae

Heritiera littoralis   Looking-glass Mangrove

It is the leaves of this mangrove which give the common name. A neat ellipsoid shape, they are clothed on the underside with minute umbrella-shaped scales, most of them silver but a few brown; this gives the undersurface a silvery sheen. Leaves on mature trees are 12-20 cm long and 5-10 cm wide, but on young plants they may be much larger, 35 cm or so, and very handsome.

Looking-glass Mangroves are typically found at the landward part of the mangrove community, and will grow away from the usual mangrove environment in sandy intertidal areas. There are some fine specimens at the Lindeman Island resort. In a swampy position they develop very prominent plank buttresses.

The small orange flowers are produced in loose, short sprays. Distinctive keeled fruits, about 8 cm long, are formed in clusters of up to five from each flower. Each contains a single seed which is edible but not delicious.

See also in chapter 6, "Flotsam".

Heritiera littoralis (Looking-glass Mangrove)

Family Verbenaceae

Avicennia eucalyptifolia   Eucalypt Mangrove

There are two species of *Avicennia* in Australia. The geographical range of the two overlaps in the Mackay area, and from here *A. marina* var. *australasica* extends south to Vïctoria while *A. eucalyptifolia* extends north to Cape York.

The two species are very similar in appearance, the most obvious difference concerning the bark, which is finely fissured and relatively rough in *A. marina* var. *australasica*, but sheds in flakes and is much smoother in *A. eucalyptifolia*.

Both species have opposite leaves but those of *A. eucalyptifolia* are a little more slender than in the southern species, the leaf blade being mostly three to four times as long as broad and 1.5–3 cm broad. The undersurface of the leaf is pale grey, or slightly yellowish in the case of young leaves, due to the presence of a dense felt of erect hairs.

Inconspicuous orange-yellow, four-petalled flowers are borne in tight groups on stalks arising from the upper leaf axils, in some cases the terminal shoot ending in a group of flowers.

Roots radiate from the base of the trunk well beyond the edge of the canopy. These travel horizontally below the

Avicennia eucalyptifolia (Eucalypt Mangrove)

surface but their path can be traced, at least in the case of isolated trees, by the lines of cobbler's peg pneumatophores. These are pencil-like erect roots produced at intervals and projecting 5–30 cm above the mud. It is these roots which allow for the aeration of the under-mud root system and so enable the plant to grow in mud in which there is commonly no free oxygen. Over the surface of the pneumatophores are lenticels, pore-like structures partly blocked by a loose mass of cork cells; these loose cells prevent entry of water but not of air. After a period of submergence, the gaseous pressure in the under-mud root system falls so that when the pneumatophores emerge on a falling tide air rushes in through the lenticels, restoring the pressure and aerating the root system.

See also in chapter 6, "Flotsam".

Sea-grasses

Sea-grasses are so called because many of them have ribbon-like, grassy leaves, although there are some in which there is no resemblance to a grass. None is a true grass.

As is the case with mangroves, they comprise a group of plants treated together because of the habitat they have occupied. However, they are not as taxonomically diverse as are the mangroves, and in the Great Barrier Reef area only three families, all monocotyledonous, have contributed to the sea-grasses.

All have prostrate stems buried in sand or mud and produce leaves on erect branches which vary in length from less than a millimetre to half a metre or more. In most cases the base of the leaf is much broadened and folded in on each side to form a sheath enclosing the lower part of the next leaf; in some species this persists after the leaf blade has been shed. Since the mud in which some of the sea-grasses grow is devoid of free oxygen, it is not surprising that there are generally well-developed air channels in leaves and stems, providing a means whereby oxygen may reach the buried parts of the plant.

Sea-grasses are common plants along quiet shores of both the mainland and the islands but are absent from the reef flat of Heron Island, being represented in that area only by deep-water plants. Although they colonize sandy positions, there is often a tendency for the habitat they occupy to become progressively muddier as underground parts decay, and as fine sediment trapped by the leaves enters the substrate.

Sea-grass beds are important in the ecosystem, providing shelter for many animals, including young fish, and food for others including some fish, swans and dugongs.

Family Cymodoceaceae

Cymodocea serrulata

Erect shoots bear up to five closely placed, ribbon-like curved leaves, 6–15 cm long and 4–9 mm wide, with finely toothed rounded apices. There are thirteen to seventeen longitudinal veins, and a distinctly triangular, purplish leaf sheath.

A second species, *Cymodocea rotundata*, is similar in general appearance to *C. serrulata*, but has narrower leaves, 2–4 mm wide, and sheaths which are not distinctly triangular and which tend to persist after the leaf blade has been shed.

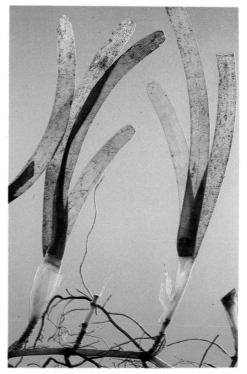

Cymodocea serrulata

Halodule uninervis

The very short, erect branches bear up to four ribbon-like leaves, 5–15 cm long and 0.3–3 mm wide, each with three longitudinal veins. At the apex, the midrib broadens and darkens, sometimes ending in a blunt tooth. At each side of the apex is a prominent tooth, and these serve to distinguish plants of this species from small specimens of *Zostera capricorni* which they superficially resemble.

A second, less common species, *Halodule pinifolia*, can be distinguished from *H. uninervis* by the presence of several small teeth on the leaf apex.

Examination of the stomach contents of Dugong in the Townsville region revealed that species of *Halodule* were the sea-grasses most heavily grazed by these mammals. The genus next in importance was *Cymodocea*, while *Halophila* and *Zostera* were present only in small quantity.

Halodule uninervis

Syringodium isoetifolium

Leaves are borne in clusters on short erect branches. The cylindrical leaf blade is 10–30 cm long, 1–2 mm broad and has a ring of six to eight air spaces running longitudinally through it. As this is the only sea-grass of the area with cylindrical leaf blades it is readily recognized.

Thalassodendron ciliatum
(Cymodocea ciliata)

Erect branches in this species are relatively long, 10–65 cm in length, and have the leaves crowded near the apex. Curved, ribbon-like leaves, 6–10 mm wide, have from seventeen to twenty-seven longitudinal veins and rounded apices with fine teeth. The plants are found mainly below low-water mark.

In general appearance, plants of *Thalassodendron ciliatum* resemble robust specimens of *Cymodocea serrulata* but can be distinguished immediately by the presence of four ring-shaped scars on the prostrate axis between successive erect shoots; there are no scars between branches in *Cymodocea*.

Family Hydrocharitaceae

Enhalus acoroides

This is the largest and coarsest of the sea-grasses in the area, the strap-like leaves, 1.3–1.7 cm broad, sometimes reaching a metre or more in length. Strong fibres in the lower part of the leaf persist, after most of the leaf has decayed, as a shaggy layer of coarse black bristles on the prostrate or shortly ascending stems. The presence of these bristles readily distinguishes *Enhalus acoroides* from all other sea-grasses in the area. The fruit, about 6 cm long, is covered with black forked bristles and borne on a long helically twisted stalk. Aborigines ate the fruit after baking it.

Enhalus acoroides

Halophila ovalis

Halophila ovalis is a distinctive sea-grass without the grassy leaves of the majority of species. The leaves arise in pairs, apparently directly from the slender creeping axis, but actually from an extremely short lateral branch enclosed in a pair of membranous scales. There is a slender leaf stalk topped with a more or less elliptical, bright green leaf blade 1–4 cm long

Halophila ovalis

and 0.5–2 cm wide. From each side of the midrib arise ten to twenty-five lateral veins, some of them forked, which join a longitudinal vein close to the margin.

The reduced flowers are borne on the short lateral branches, the male flowers on slender stalks, the females stalkless. Pollen grains are rounded, not filamentous as are those of *Zostera*, but since they are united in chains they also are well adapted to catching against the slender stigmas of the female flowers.

H. minor (H. ovata) is very similar to *H. ovalis* but the plants are generally smaller, with leaves not over 5 mm wide, and are distinguished more clearly by having usually only four to ten unforked veins on each side of the midrib.

H. decipiens also has the general appearance of *H. ovalis* but is distinguished by its finely serrate leaf margins and, generally, by the presence of a few projecting hairs on one or both leaf surfaces. In the Great Barrier Reef area this species has been found at depths of over 50 m.

Halophila spinulosa

This species bears little resemblance to the three species of the genus noted above but is equally distinctive and easily recognized. Erect shoots, up to about 15 cm long, bear up to

Halophila spinulosa

twenty pairs of obliquely arranged leaves in one plane, each leaf up to 2.5 cm long and 5 mm broad. These erect leafy branches have something of the appearance of a pinnate fern frond.

Plants of *Halophila spinulosa* are found mainly below low-water mark and, on the Great Barrier Reef, have been collected at depths of up to 45 m.

Thalassia hemprichii

Short erect branches bear a cluster of curved, strap-like leaves mostly 10–30 cm long and 4–11 mm wide, with ten to seventeen longitudinal veins. Prominent fruits are borne on stalks which raise them hardly above the surface of the sand; they are mostly 2–3 cm broad, globose-conical, coarsely hairy, and are marked by eight to twenty longitudinal lines along which the fruit eventually splits into valves which bend back, releasing the seeds.

This sea-grass appears to be intolerant of lowered salinities, and it is possibly because of this that it seems to be restricted to the vicinity of islands where freshwater runoff is relatively minor. In some of these situations it is the dominant sea-grass on reef flats but it may also descend to depths of several metres.

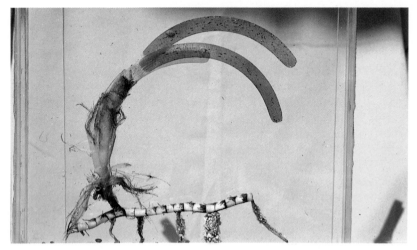

Thalassia hemprichii

The sea-grass with which *Thalassia hemprichii* is most likely to be confused is *Cymodocea serrulata*. These species are distinguishable by the fact that *Cymodocea* has a ligule, a small flap of tissue at the junction of leaf blade and leaf sheath, while there is no such structure in *Thalassia*. Also, in the latter genus there are several scars on the prostrate axis between successive erect branches but none in *Cymodocea*.

Family Zosteraceae

Zostera capricorni   Eel-grass

Each of the short erect branches produces a group of up to six ribbon-like leaves 2–5 mm wide and from a few centimetres to half a metre in length. There are usually five main longitudinal veins, all linking near the apex where the midvein is dilated and darkened. (Species of *Halodule* which may be superficially similar have only three veins). The apex generally has a cut-off appearance and may bear a few irregular, microscopic teeth.

During spring and summer, erect leafy branches up to 50 cm long are produced, and it is on these branches that the flowers are borne. Both male and female flowers are minute reduced structures borne in a group of seven to ten of each sex and enclosed in a membranous sheath. Pollen is very unusual in that it is filamentous. The grains are carried by water currents and some, by chance, catch against the extremely slender protruding stigmas of the female flowers.

Zostera capricorni is a widespread species in Australia, and in many places in the lower intertidal region and at depths of up to 6 m forms dense marine meadows completely obscuring the substrate.

Black Swans can often be seen working over *Zostera* beds to which they may do considerable damage, stripping leaves and eating the prostrate stems.

Zostera capricorni (Eel-grass)

6 *Flotsam*

The continental islands and the cays of the Great Barrier Reef Province differ both in their own origins and in the origins of their floras. The continental islands, such as those of the Whitsunday Group, were once part of the mainland, and became separated from it through a rise in the sea level. As they became islands they carried their flora with them. Because of their relatively recent status as islands and their closeness to the mainland they have not developed a distinctive endemic flora as have islands, such as those of Hawaii, which have been isolated over a long period and by great distances from major plant communities. However, the cays, which have been islands throughout their existence, owe their flora to transport of seeds and fruits, together sometimes known as propagules, over an ocean barrier. The effectiveness of this barrier to the migration of propagules varies with factors such as the distance from an established flora, and the direction of the prevailing winds and water currents. This barrier, together with the relatively limited range of habitats available on a cay, results in the flora of a cay being very limited in number of species, often no more than about fifty.

There are three ways in which propagules may cross the ocean barrier: they may be carried by animals, blown by the wind, or carried by ocean or tidal currents.

Apart from people, who have distributed species to cays both deliberately and accidentally, the only animals involved in distribution of seeds to cays are birds. They may carry propagules embedded in mud on their feet, sticking to feathers, or in the intestinal tract. Fig trees, for example, have almost certainly reached Great Barrier Reef cays as propagules carried internally by birds, while the sticky fruits of *Pisonia grandis* are particularly well adapted to being carried attached to feathers. Among species occupying the central part of a cay with a well-established flora there is usually a high proportion dispersed by birds.

For successful aerial transport a propagule needs a large surface area in relation to its volume. This is achieved in some plants, such as the orchids, by the production of extremely small seeds, in others by the production of wings or plumes which greatly increase the surface area while adding relatively little weight. Milk Thistles, with their delicately plumed fruits, probably reached the cays carried by wind. Transport by wind over a wide ocean barrier of hundreds of thousands of kilometres has a much reduced chance of success because of the increased likelihood of the propagule coming down in the sea at some stage with no chance of becoming airborne again.

Successful transport by sea requires two important attributes in the propagule, buoyancy and, except in the case of mangroves, protection of the embryo from the damaging effect of salt water. Species able to establish themselves after transport in this way are mainly those which are well adapted to colonizing the difficult habitat presented on arrival by a sandy shore just above high-water mark, where the sand is infertile, non-retentive, unstable and subject to a heavy salt drift from the ocean. The majority of species occupying the marginal areas of the cays reached this position originally through ocean transport, and nearly all of them are widespread in the western Pacific Ocean, many extending also to the Indian Ocean. In fact, the vegetation on sand bordering the beach is much the same whether the site is on a continent, continental island or cay.

Arrival of a water-borne propagule on a beach does not necessarily lead to successful establishment. Fruits or seeds of some rainforest trees such as *Castanospermum australe* (Moreton Bay Chestnut, Black Bean) are dispersed by the sea, but are deposited in an environment so different from the moist, shaded rainforest and creek bank where they are usually found that they have only a slight chance of establishing after sea dispersal. Propagules of other species are carried well beyond their geographical range; viable seeds of *Barringtonia asiatica* (Box Fruit) and *Calophyllum inophyllum* (Alexandrian Laurel) reach shores south of the Tropic of Capricorn but the species do not become established there, probably because they are unable to tolerate winter temperatures at that latitude. Many propagules make landfall only after long periods at sea, during which their embryos lose their viability either through ageing or through damage by penetrating sea water; coconuts washed up on southern beaches are generally non-viable.

Shores of the Great Barrier Reef Province are a beachcomber's delight. Although it is the great variety of shells and the remains, in various stages of erosion, of other reef animals which excite most interest, the wide variety and relatively large size of many of the drift seeds and fruits of tropical shores certainly add greatly to the interest of pottering along the drift lines. Some are freshly shed, only a few days old, others are covered by small encrusting animals or support Goose Barnacles indicating a long period of ocean travel, possibly from shores beyond Australia.

It is not possible in this section to deal with all the plant material which will be found from time to time among the flotsam of the Great Barrier Reef Province. There are numerous species, such as *Argusia argentea* and *Sophora tomentosa*, which have sea-dispersed propagules but which are relatively small and likely to be noted only by someone making a careful search of the drift line. There are others, usually found in small numbers, originating in Australian rainforests or from beyond Australia, and many of these, with the present state of knowledge, are difficult to determine. The material dealt with here concerns, in the main, the larger of the common propagules effectively dispersed by oceans, although a few distinctive exceptions to this category and a few of the more durable of the drift algae are also included.

Division Chlorophyta

Halimeda opuntia

This species is one of the commonest and most heavily calcified of the Green Algae. Green or grey-green when fresh,
plants quickly bleach in the sun, and pure white clumps of
the kidney-shaped or trilobed flattened segments are often
common where they have been tossed by storms above the
normal level of high tides.

See also in chapter 2, "Seaweeds".

Halimeda opuntia

Division Phaeophyta

Sargassum   Sargassum

At some periods, each wave as it recedes leaves on the beach a sinuate brown line made up of small vesicles 2–5 mm across. These are not the ocean-dispersed seeds of a flowering plant but are floats derived from seaweeds of the genus *Sargassum* from which they are shed in large numbers as the plants start to deteriorate.

See also in chapter 2, "Seaweeds".

Sargassum sp. – vesicles stranded on the beach

Division Rhodophyta

Galaxaura

Most seaweeds washed up on the beach quickly shrink and decay, but plants of species of the Red Algal genus *Galaxaura* are calcified and so are relatively durable. They bleach to a pure white which makes the tufts of repeatedly forked cylindrical branches conspicuous items in the uppermost drift lines.

Species of *Amphiroa* also are calcified, and bleached specimens may superficially resemble those of *Galaxaura*. However, they are less commonly found intact because the numerous uncalcified joints lead to dried speciments fragmenting readily.

See also in chapter 2, "Seaweeds".

Galaxaura sp. – bleached specimen on beach

Family Anacardiaceae

Pleiogynium timorense   Burdekin Plum

Burdekin Plum is a widely distributed tree in tropical Queensland and not one particularly characteristic of the coast. The fruits are flattened-globose with a thin, purple edible flesh surrounding the woody stone, which is the part sometimes found among drift lines. This stone is broadly and irregularly top-shaped and 2–3 cm across. Its sides are irregularly furrowed, and the broad end carries twelve to fourteen prominent pits rounds its margin. Many of the specimens found on the beach do not float and it is unlikely that ocean transport is an important means of dispersal for this species.

Pleiogynium timorense (Burdekin Plum)

Family Apocynaceae

Cerbera manghas   Dog Bane

The elliptical, slightly flattened fruits, 6–8 cm long, have a thin fleshy layer which decays quickly, leaving a network of longitudinal fibrous strands exposed. Once these have worn away the two pithy, roughened, slightly diverging halves of the inner fruit are revealed.

See also in chapter 4, "Plants of the Shore".

Cerbera manghas (Dog Bane)

Ochrosia cowleyi

The drift fruits of this species resemble those of *Cerbera manghas,* being flattened-elliptical, 6–7 cm long, split into two slightly diverging halves and covered with closely appressed fibrous strands. They differ from the fruits of *C. manghas* in having much tougher strands which branch but do not form a network as do those of *C. manghas.* In the latter species the lower strands originate from the central point of the lower end but in *Ochrosia cowleyi* they originate to one side of centre giving the structure a vaguely animal-like appearance. There is some doubt as to the correct name to be applied to this species.

Ochrosia cowleyi

Family Arecaceae (Palmae)

Cocos nucifera   Coconut

The coconut is the best known of all the water-dispersed fruits. Except for the fruit of the remarkable Double Coconut or Coco-de-mer (*Lodoicea maldivica*) of the Seychelles Archipelago, it is also the largest fruit and seed so dispersed. The fruit reaches a diameter of about 20 cm, and beneath the tough, shiny outer layer is a thick fibrous husk which is the part mainly responsible for the buoyancy, and which is the source of coir used in door mats and for coarse ropes. Before sale, the fibrous layer is commonly removed revealing the very hard, bony inner shell which has often been used in the Indo–Pacific area for making utensils. At one end of the shell are three holes which impart a face-like apperance; through one of them the first root and leaf appear.

There has been some controversy over whether or not the coconut fruit is as effective a body in dispersal as its structure would suggest. Although one experiment indicated that immersion for a month was likely to destroy the viability of some nuts, another experiment showed that a coconut could germinate after 110 days in the sea. They have been found to remain afloat, although not viable, for at least 214 days, and it is estimated that they are capable of travelling about 5000 km.

See also in chapter 4, "Plants of the Shore".

Cocos nucifera (Coconut)

Family Caesalpiniaceae

Caesalpinia bonduc   Nicker Nut, Wait-a-while

The shiny, grey, almost porcelain-like seeds of *Caesalpinia bonduc* are sometimes used effectively in necklaces. They are rounded-angular, 1.5–2 cm across, with a very hard shell. There is a brown spot marking the point at which the seed was attached in the pod, and surrounding this are fine concentric rings extending over the whole seed.

The seeds are capable of remaining afloat for long periods, and specimens originating in the West Indies region have reached Scandinavian shores. Experiments have shown the seeds capable of floating in sea water for two and a half years; some seeds which were planted after one year's immersion germinated.

Buoyancy is due generally to a large air space between the cotyledons, or seed-leaves, but in some seeds there may also be some space between the seed-coat and the cotyledons.

See also in chapter 4, "Plants of the Shore".

Caesalpinia bonduc (Nicker Nut)

Cynometra iripa   Wrinkle-pod Mangrove
(*C. ramiflora* var. *bijuga*)

Fruits of *Cynometra iripa* could easily be disregarded as non-descript pieces of debris. They are roughly kidney-shaped and have a deeply wrinkled surface. The pithy wall, up to 5 mm thick in parts, is responsible for buoyancy; it contains a single seed.

See also in chapter 5, "Flowering Plants in the Sea".

Cynometra iripa (Wrinkle-pod Mangrove)

Intsia bijuga   Queensland Teak, Johnstone River Teak

The flattened, dark brown seeds of this species might be mistaken for small specimens of *Entada phaseoloides*. They tend to be more irregular in outline and are more compressed, as well as smaller, up to 4 cm long and 6 mm thick. When freshly shed, the seeds have a rusty-brown furry coating but this is easily rubbed off to leave the dull blackish-brown seedcoat.

Buoyancy is due to the light weight of the seed-leaf tissues.
See also in chapter 4, "Plants of the Shore".

Intsia bijuga (Queensland Teak)

Family Casuarinaceae

Casuarina equisetifolia var. *incana*   Coastal Sheoak

Trees of the Coastal Sheoak often overhang the intertidal beach so it is not surprising that its rounded, spiky cones, about 1.5 cm across, are common among the debris of drift lines. However, these opened cones play no part in dispersal of the species, the small winged nuts being shed before the cones leave the tree.

See also in chapter 4, "Plants of the Shore".

Casuarina equisetifolia var. *incana* (Coastal Sheoak)

Family Chrysobalanaceae

Parinari glaberrimum

This species is not known to occur in Australia, so the large fruits washed up on Australian shores are well travelled, probably originating from islands in the Pacific. The fruits are elliptical or egg-shaped, sometimes slightly flattened, about 8 cm long, and have a tough shell, 5–10 cm thick, enclosing a single seed. A compact tissue of fibres, arranged at right-angles to the surface, makes up the shell, and this arrangement leads to the development of numerous irregular cracks in the shell as it dries out after being stranded. At one time, the natives of Fiji obtained a perfume from the seed which they also beat into a putty for caulking canoes and fixing spear heads to hafts.

Parinari glaberrimum

Family Clusiaceae (Guttiferae)

Calophyllum inophyllum   Alexandrian Laurel

Once the fruit is shed the thin, grey-green, fleshy layer wrinkles and turns brown. In the sea this outer layer is lost, a few encircling fibrous strands from the base being the last to go. The hard, light-brown shell then revealed is only slightly roughened, 3–4 cm across, almost globose but usually with a small beak at the stalk end. The fruits have been found to float for four months but their viability after immersion does not seem to have been tested.

Buoyancy is due to the oily nature of the seed and to air-containing tissue between the shell and seed.

See also in chapter 4, "Plants of the Shore".

Calophyllum inophyllum (Alexandrian Laurel)

Family Combretaceae

Terminalia catappa   Sea Almond, Indian Almond

The more or less almond-shaped fruits have a distinct marginal flange and are up to 10 cm long. There is an outer, fleshy purplish layer attractive to bats, and it has been reported that in South-East Asia *Terminalia catappa* is dispersed by these animals. Within the fleshy layer, which quickly rots off in the water, is a thick buoyant corky-fibrous layer enclosing a single, elongate, relatively small seed. This buoyant layer gradually wears away leaving an often shaggy structure marked with the remains of transverse vascular strands. Fruits can remain afloat for at least two years.

Smaller fruits of this type belong to other species of *Terminalia*, particularly *T. arenicola*.

See also in chapter 4, "Plants of the Shore".

Terminalia arenicola (Beach Almond)

Family Elaeocarpaceae

Elaeocarpus grandis   Blue Quandong

Spherical structures about 2 cm across, with deep, labyrinthine pits are the fruits of *Elaeocarpus grandis* from which the blue fleshy layer has rotted away. *E. grandis* is a rainforest tree, and although its fruits are sometimes dispersed by ocean currents it is unlikely that this dispersal often leads to the establishment of seedlings.

Elaeocarpus grandis (Blue Quandong)

Family Euphorbiaceae

Aleurites moluccana   Candle-nut

Candle-nut is a tropical rainforest tree rather than a species of the shores, but the walnut-sized seeds are not infrequently cast up in drift material after being carried down rivers to the ocean. The common name of Fossil Prune, used in some parts of the United States, suggests the appearance; the seed has a very hard, somewhat wrinkled shell, is generally flattened-rounded but with a protruding point, and becomes black in drift.

Only empty or nearly empty seeds of Candle-nut float, so drift seeds are seldom viable, and ocean currents cannot be regarded as a means of dispersal for the species.

Aleurites moluccana (Candle-nut)

Family Fabaceae

Castanospermum australe   Moreton Bay Chestnut
                                             Black Bean

The Moreton Bay Chestnut is a familiar tree in Queensland, with its glossy pinnate leaves and its summer masses of showy orange and yellow flowers which attract flocks of parrots to their abundant nectar supply. It is not typically a tree of the strand, but grows in rainforests, especially along the banks of rivers and creeks. The fruit is a large, thick pod up to 25 cm long, but light, with a copious layer of pithy tissue surrounding usually two to four seeds. When the pods fall into the water they are carried downstream, sometimes to a suitable riverbank site, but frequently out to sea, and thus may be cast up in drift.

Pods twist slightly as they split open to reveal the glossy brown seeds similar to large chestnuts in size and appearance. The seed has a thin coat surrounding two very thick white seed-leaves packed with starch; although they look attractive as food, they are poisonous unless treated by a lengthy process of pounding, soaking and baking as was done by the Aborigines.

Although only the pods float, shed seeds are often found in drift. Empty half-pods make excellent toy boats.

Castanospermum australe (Moreton Bay Chestnut)

Mucuna gigantea   Velvet Bean

Velvet Bean seeds stand out among the material on the shore as smooth black discs 2–3 cm in diameter, their circular outline marred by a bulge on one side caused by the root of the embryo inside. The girdle of the seed is marked by a lighter scar, the hilum, which extends around more than three-quarters of the circumference; the hilum is the area of attachment of the seed to its stalk when inside the pod.

Tissues of the seed-leaves are very light and are responsible for the buoyancy of the seeds. This is one of the species in which germination may commence in sea water at high temperatures, resulting in death of the embryo if it is not soon removed from the sea.

Powdered seeds have been doubtfully reported to have aphrodisiac properties, and are more reliably known as a purgative. Refer to page 273 illustration.

See also in chapter 4, "Plants of the Shore".

Family Lauraceae

Cryptocarya glabella   Poison Walnut
(C. pleurosperma)

Poison Walnut is a rainforest tree notorious for the painful blistering caused by skin contact with its irritant sap. It is not known to be effectively dispersed by the sea, but the very distinctive elliptical stones, approximately 3 cm across with about twelve prominent longitudinal ridges, are sometimes washed up on beaches.

Cryptocarya glabella (Poison Walnut)

Family Lecythidaceae

Barringtonia asiatica   Box Fruit

Next to the coconut this is the largest of the fruits normally found on Great Barrier Reef beaches. It is somewhat top-shaped in outline but very distinctly four-angled, and occasionally five- or six-angled. There is a shiny, almost papery outer layer which in many drift specimens has been partly eroded to reveal the thick, buoyant fibrous layer beneath. Fruits are known to float for up to two years. The fruits have been used for fish-net floats in some areas while the single large seed has been grated or pounded by native peoples for use as fish poison.

See also in chapter 4, "Plants of the Shore".

Barringtonia asiatica (Box Fruit)

Barringtonia racemosa

This is a tree of swampy localities, producing fruits mostly 4–6 cm long, elliptical in outline, and distinctly four-angled particularly near the upper end. Once the thin outer layer disappears a loose network of fibres is seen surrounding a fragile, almost papery shell.

Barringtonia racemosa

Family Liliaceae

Crinum pedunculatum   Crinum Lily

Shiny green fruits of the Crinum Lily eventually turn brown and split to release a few rounded-angular, fleshy seeds up to 3 cm.across. These are unusual in possessing no seed-coat, but a thin, grey-green corky surface layer gives some protection. Seeds germinate readily when stranded above normal high-water mark, gradually shrivelling as the developing shoot and root draw nutrients from it.

See also in chapter 4, "Plants of the Shore".

Crinum pedunculatum (Crinum Lily)

Family Meliaceae

Xylocarpus granatum   Cannonball Tree

Seeing the cannonball fruit hanging from a tree of *Xylocarpus granatum* gives little clue to the identity of its angular, corky seeds, up to 8 cm across, when washed up on the beach. In many specimens there is a rough, stubby outgrowth which appears to be a stalk but which is the first root. It is reported that seeds of this species sometimes germinate while still floating, an unusual occurrence among species dispersed by ocean currents.

Buoyancy is due to numerous small air spaces in the corky seed-coat which in some parts is up to 1 cm thick.

See also in chapter 5, "Flowering Plants in the Sea".

Xylocarpus granatum (Cannonball Tree)

Family Mimosaceae

Entada phaseoloides   Matchbox Bean

When the large pods of Matchbox Bean break up on the vine, segments of pod, each containing a single seed, may be shed. These segments are fairly fragile, and more usually it is the seed alone which is found. The seeds are typically flattened discs 4.5–6 cm in diameter and 1.5–2 cm thick, but there is considerable variation with some seeds much smaller, and many tending to have two straight sides. Fresh seeds are a glossy chocolate brown. An air space between the seed leaves provides buoyancy.

The seeds have had several uses. Being ornamental, they have been made into small boxes for matches or snuff; the starch in them has been used for food but only after the toxic principles have been washed out; medicinally they have been used as a purgative and an emetic, and have had an unproven reputation as a contraceptive.

See also in chapter 4, "Plants of the Shore".

Entada phaseoloides, a smaller seed of *Mucuna gigantea* and a piece of bleached *Halimeda opuntia*

Family Myrsinaceae

Aegiceras corniculatum   River Mangrove

Although this mangrove does not belong to the Rhizophora-
ceae, it shares with members of that family the viviparous
habit, and produces a somewhat similar seedling. In this case
the hypocotyl is comparatively small, about 3 cm long, and
strongly curved, so the seedlings may be recognized as small
yellowish-green horns among the drift.

See also chapter 5, "Flowering Plants in the Sea".

Aegiceras corniculatum (River Mangrove)

Family Pandanaceae

Pandanus   Screw Pine

Pandanus fruits are cone-like structures, often about head size, consisting of numerous segments or syncarps which generally separate from each other and fall individually when ripe. The wedge-shaped syncarp has several knobs on the broad end, and a brush-like tuft of fibres at the other end.

Oily seeds occur in individual cavities in a woody structure surrounded by a pithy-fibrous layer which gives the structure its buoyancy. Abrasion on the beach eventually removes the fibrous layer and reduces the central woody part to an irregular disc penetrated by several holes which, at first sight, is not readily identifiable as *Pandanus*.

See also in chapter 4, "Plants of the Shore".

Pandanus sp. (Screw Pine)

Family Rhizophoraceae

Bruguiera gymnorhiza   Orange Mangrove

Among the most eye-catching specimens in the drift are the apple-red spent flowers of the Orange Mangrove, shaped like bells with a fringe of rigid claws.

Developed seedlings occur also, with a cigar-shaped hypocotyl topped by a small shoot. Distinctive ribbing of the hypocotyl enables easy recognition of seedlings of the related *Bruguiera exaristata*.

See also in chapter 5, "Flowering Plants in the Sea".

Bruguiera gymnorhiza (Orange Mangrove)

Ceriops tagal   Yellow Mangrove

The seedling of *Ceriops tagal* has a general resemblance to those of the more conspicuous *Rhizophora* and *Bruguiera*, being an elongate club-shaped hypocotyl with a small conical shoot and small root at the other end. They may be distinguished by their size: although up to 20 cm long, they are only about 1 cm thick.

See also in chapter 5, "Flowering Plants in the Sea".

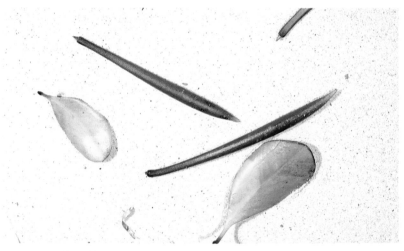

Ceriops tagal (Yellow Mangrove)

Rhizophora   Spider Mangrove, Stilt Mangrove

Seedlings of the various species of *Rhizophora* are produced while the fruit is still on the tree. Shed in great numbers from the large mangrove forests, these seedlings may form a conspicuous part of the drift flora. Elongate, often curved clubs up to 50 cm long consist mostly of hypocotyl containing air spaces which enable the seedling to float; at the upper end is

Rhizophora stylosa (Spider Mangrove)

a small conical shoot, while at the base the hypocotyl grades into a short root.

Fruits of *Rhizophora* are less obvious, but are not uncommon. They have the appearance of a small upside-down pear.

See also in chapter 5, "Flowering Plants in the Sea".

Family Rubiaceae

Guettarda speciosa

Fruits of *Guettarda speciosa*, once they lose their thin outer coat, are rounded and somewhat flattened, about 2.5 cm across, and loosely enveloped by fibrous strands attached near the base. As these strands wear or rot away, the inner part of the fruit is seen to be distinctly five-lobed, with a deep hole in the middle of each groove. Small air spaces within the tough, spongy five-lobed structure are responsible for keeping the fruit afloat for at least fifty days.

See also in chapter 4, "Plants of the Shore".

Guettarda speciosa

Family Sterculiaceae

Heritiera littoralis   Looking-glass Mangrove

Fruits of the Looking-glass Mangrove resemble small, keeled boats and are 6–10 cm long. The shell, shiny and brown in fresh specimens, dull and greyish in well-weathered ones, is buoyant, and the space between shell and seed provides extra flotation. Many shells carry round shot-holes through which insects that have destroyed the seed have emerged.

See also in chapter 5, "Flowering Plants in the Sea".

Heritiera littoralis (Looking-glass Mangrove)

Family Verbenaceae

Avicennia eucalyptifolia   Eucalypt Mangrove

The fruit is a flattened, yellow-green capsule densely covered with short hairs. There is a single seed which lacks a seed-coat so that peeling off the thin fruit wall reveals the two dark green, fleshy, folded seed leaves. At the end of the well-developed hypocotyl is a tuft of brown, reflexed hairs which have been suggested as being an aid to attachment of the seedling in the mud. Once the structure is stranded in a suitable position a ring of fleshy white roots develops from among the brown hairs. Tests have shown that the seedlings of at least one species of *Avicennia* are very hardy, recovering after drying for twenty-five days at room temperature.

The fleshy cotyledons have been used as food by the Aborigines, but neither boiling nor baking removes the bitter flavour which reduce their attraction as food.

See also in chapter 5, "Flowering Plants in the Sea".

Avicennia sp.

Glossary
of technical terms

agar Gelatinous product of certain Red Algae

alternate (leaves) Produced singly on stem; cf. opposite

anther Part of flower producing pollen; usually yellow, often lobed

appressed Pressed closely against surface

axil Angle between stem and leaf

axillary In leaf axil

axis Central supporting structure, often stem-like

basal At base

bract Specialized leaf associated with flowers; in some cases coloured and showy, resembling a petal

buttress Projection from lower trunk of tree; often of fairly even thickness, then "plank buttress"

calcareous Stony or chalky due to abundance of lime

calcified Containing lime but not necessarily stony

calyx Sepals collectively; outermost protective part of flower, usually green

cartilaginous Like cartilage, firm but flexible

cay Small island associated with coral reef and generally built mainly from remains of calcareous animals and plants

character Feature of plant or plant group

compound (leaf) With blade divided into two or more separate leaflets (compound leaf distinguished from branch by presence of bud at base in axil)

coralline	In this work referring to a group of heavily calcified Red Algae
corolla	Petals, collectively
cotyledon	Seed-leaf (embryo in seed of flowering plant bearing one or two cotyledons, and such plants grouped accordingly as mono-cotyledons or dicotyledons)
determination	Application of correct name to specimen
detritus	Mass of fine broken-down material
discoid	Rounded and flat, disc-shaped
elliptical	With shape of an ellipse; elongate with rounded ends, the two ends symmetrical
emetic	Inducing vomiting
epiphyte	Plant growing on another, using it as support only and not growing as a parasite
exudate	Liquid flowing from plant either from gland or from injury
filament	Thread-like body (many algae of basically filamentous construction)
floret	Small flower, especially a single flower of many making up the head of a daisy or similar plant
garden escape	Cultivated plant growing for several generations in the wild but without becoming fully established and naturalized as a weed
glycoside	Naturally occurring compound made up of a sugar with some other chemical; some of medicinal use, some poisonous
hypocotyl	Portion of seedling between stem and root; in some plants important for storage of starch and other reserve materials
inflorescence	Group of flowers borne on a plant; arrangement of individual flowers on a plant
latex	White fluid exuded from some plants on injury
lenticel	Pocket of corky cells on woody stem or root allowing exchange of gases between interior of plant and atmosphere
ligule	Outgrowth, frequently flap of tissue, at junction of leaf blade and leaf base on some plants, especially grasses
lithothamnia	Heavily calcified Red Algae growing mainly as a crust over substrates such as rock and dead coral

monocotyledonous	Belonging to the monocotyledons, plants with single seed-leaf in the embryo; such plants usually with parallel veins in the leaves and with the parts of the flowers in threes or multiples of three, e.g., grasses, palms, lilies
mucilaginous	Slimy
obovate	Egg-shaped in outline, with broader end at apex
opposite (leaves)	Produced in pairs at same level on stem but on opposite sides, cf. alternate
ovary	Female organ of flower, situated in centre of flower and developing into fruit containing seeds
ovate	Egg-shaped in outline, with broader end at base
palmate or palmately compound (leaves)	Compound and having number of leaflets radiating from a common point
pea-flower	Typical flower of Family Fabaceae (peas, beans) with five petals − large standard at back, two wings at sides, and two petals united to form protruding keel enclosing stamens and ovary
pinnate (leaves)	Compound and having number of leaflets produced from central axis or rib as in a feather
plumose	Like plumes or ostrich feathers
pneumatophore	Erect root protruding above substrate, bearing numerous lenticels allowing gas exchange between root and atmosphere
polyp	Individual animal of coral
province	Region characterized by relatively distinct and homogeneous flora and fauna
pulvinus	Swollen leaf base; in some cases responsible for movement of the leaf
ret	Prepare fibres from plant material by soaking and allowing soft tissues to decay
rhizoid	Fine root-like structure found in non-flowering plants
saponin	Naturally occurring chemical made up of a sugar and some other substance, frothing when shaken with water; some poisonous
scale	Reduced leaf, without chlorophyll and therefore not green

sepal	Member of calyx, outermost part of flower; usually green
serrate	Toothed
simple (leaf)	With blade not divided into leaflets, although sometimes lobed or toothed, cf. compound
sinuate	Winding
spike	Inflorescence of stalkless flowers carried on elongate axis
spikelet	Unit of grass inflorescence, consisting of greatly reduced flowers surrounded by scaly bracts
sporangium (pl. sporangia)	Sac containing spores
spore	Reproductive body of lower plants, usually single cell
stamen	Male organ of flower, consisting of filament (stalk) and anther containing pollen
stigma	Sticky or feathery area above ovary, receiving pollen at pollination
stipule	One of a pair of outgrowths from base of leaf or from stem close to base of leaf, taking various forms
striated	Marked with fine parallel lines, sometimes as grooves
style	Projection from top of ovary supporting stigma
substrate	Material in or on which plant is growing, e.g., soil, rock, sand
trifoliate (leaves)	Compound with three leaflets
umbel	Inflorescence of stalked flowers all arising from same point
undulate	Wavy
vesicle	Small bladder
viviparous	With seed germinating while still in fruit on the tree
whorl	Groups of three or more leaves or flower parts arranged in circle around axis

Further reading

Bennett, I. 1981. *The Great Barrier Reef.* Melbourne: Lansdowne Press.

Byrnes, N. B., Everist, S. L., Reynolds, S. T., Specht, A., and Specht, R. L. 1977. The vegetation of Lizard Island, north Queensland. *Proceedings of the Royal Society of Queensland* 88:1–15.

Cribb, A. B. 1965. The marine and terrestrial vegetation of Wilson Island, Great Barrier Reef. *Proceedings of the Royal Society of Queensland* 77:53–62, pls 2–3.

_____. 1966. The algae of Heron Island, Great Barrier Reef, Australia, part 1. A general account. *Papers of the University of Queensland Heron Island Research Station* 1 (1):1–23.

_____. 1969. The vegetation of North West Island. *The Queensland Naturalist* 19 (4–6):85–93.

_____. 1969. Algae on a Hawk's-bill Turtle. *The Queensland Naturalist* 19 (4–6):108–9.

_____. 1969. The Pisonia. *The Queensland Naturalist* 19 (4–6): 110–14.

_____. 1969. Sea sawdust. *The Queensland Naturalist* 19 (4–6): 115–17.

_____. 1972. The vegetation of Hoskyn I. and reef. *The Queensland Naturalist* 20 (4–6):92–100.

_____. 1973. The algae of the Great Barrier Reefs. In *Biology and geology of coral reefs,* vol. 2, no. 1, O. A. Jones and R. Endean, eds, pp. 47–75. New York: Academic Press.

_____. 1975. Terrestrial vegetation of Masthead Island. *The Queensland Naturalist* 21 (3–4):74–78.

_____. 1975. Algal vegetation of Masthead Island reef. *The Queensland Naturalist* 21 (3–4):79–83.

_____. 1975. Some fungi from Masthead Island. *The Queensland Naturalist* 21 (3–4):73.

_____. 1976. Changes in the terrestrial flora of Heron Island. *The Queensland Naturalist* 21 (5–6):110–12.

_____. 1978. Marine algal vegetation, Hinchinbrook Island. *The Queensland Naturalist* 22 (1–4):62–66.

_____. 1978. List of marine algae from Hinchinbrook Island. *The Queensland Naturalist* 22 (5–6):67–69.

_____. 1980. Terrestrial vegetation of Tryon Island. *The Queensland Naturalist* 22 (5–6):127–32.

_____. 1981. Coral reefs. In *Marine botany: an Australian perspective,* N. M. Clayton and R. J. King, eds, pp. 329–45. Melbourne: Longman Cheshire.

_____. 1983. Marine algae of the southern Great Barrier Reef, part 1. Rhodophyta. Brisbane: Australian Coral Reef Society.

Cribb, A. B., and Cribb, J. W. 1969. Some marine fungi from the Great Barrier Reef area. *The Queensland Naturalist* 19 (4–6):118–20.

_____. 1975. *Wild food in Australia.* Sydney: William Collins.

_____. 1981. *Useful wild plants in Australia.* Sydney: William Collins.

_____. 1981. *Wild medicine in Australia.* Sydney: William Collins.

Endean, R. 1982. *Australia's Great Barrier Reef.* St Lucia: University of Queensland Press.

Flood, P. G. 1977. Coral cays of the Capricorn and Bunker Groups, Great Barrier Reef Province, Australia. *Atoll Research Bulletin* no. 195:1–7, figs 1–8, pls 1–10.

Fosberg, F. R. 1961. Description of Heron Island. *Atoll Research Bulletin* no. 82:1–4.

Fosberg, F. R., and Thorne, R. F. 1961. Vascular plants of Heron Island. *Atoll Research Bulletin* no. 82:5–13.

Gunn, C. R., and Dennis, J. V. 1976. *World guide to tropical drift seeds and fruits.* New York: Times Books.

Guppy, H. B. 1906. *Observations of a naturalist in the Pacific between 1896 and 1899.* London: Macmillan.

Heatwole, H. 1981. *A coral island: the story of One Tree Island and its reef.* Sydney: William Collins.

Heatwole, H., Done, T., and Cameron, E. 1981. *Community ecology of a coral cay: a study of One-Tree Island, Great Barrier Reef, Australia.* The Hague: Dr W. Junk.

Lear, R. and Turner, T. 1977. *Mangroves of Australia.* St Lucia: University of Queensland Press.

Mather, P. and Bennett, I., eds 1978. *A coral reef handbook.* Brisbane: The Great Barrier Reef Committee.

Maxwell, W. G. H. 1968. *Atlas of the Great Barrier Reef.* Amsterdam: Elsevier.

Merrill, E. D. 1945. *Plant life of the Pacific world.* New York: Macmillan.

Price, I. R., Larkum, A. W. D., and Bailey, A. 1976. Check list of marine benthic plants collected in Lizard Island area. *Australian Journal of Plant Physiology* 3:3–8.

Saenger, P. 1979. Records of sub-tidal algae from the Swains Reef Complex, Great Barrier Reef, Queensland. *Proceedings of the Royal Society of Queensland* 90:51–55.

Steers, J. A. 1938. Detailed notes on the islands surveyed and examined by the geographical expedition to the Great Barrier Reef in 1936. *Report of the Great Barrier Reef Committee* 4 (3) No. 7:51–104.

Stephenson, T. A., Stephenson, A., Tandy, G., and Spender, M. 1931. The structure and ecology of Low Isles and other reefs. *Great Barrier Reef Expedition 1928–29, Scientific Reports* 3 (2):2–112, pls 1–27.

Index of scientific and common names of plants